VERBAL PLENARY PRESERVATION
AND
HUMAN RESPONSIBILITY

- THE LAW OF INALTERABILITY IN THE BIBLE -

RA CHAEWON, Ph.D.

All Glory and Praise
to God
My Lord and Everlasting Father
and the Eternal Truth

CONTENTS

INTRODUCTION

<u>Background and Problem</u>

If someone asks Christians what the only element that cannot be omitted is, it is the Bible. It is not the church building, congregations, or offerings that form the basis of Christian faith, but only the written Word of God, the Bible. The biggest problem with existing churches today is the absence of the Bible. It does not mean that there is no Bible itself, but that there is no confidence and trust in the Bible which God Himself wrote and has preserved. Today, churches seem to have their own buildings filled with congregations and raise their operational funds through the offerings from their congregations. However, God's Word, which should be there, is relatively devalued or neglected from the outset. And this ultimately results in the absence of the Bible within the churches; they use and read the Bible, but there is no conviction that it is 'the' Bible, which has been preserved by God Himself, the very same as the originals (autographs) written by God's inspiration. This absence of confidence in God's written Word, the Bible, has a fatal effect on confidence and trust in the words that are preached. Even if the preacher studies and preaches God's Word, it leaves some room for doubt because he is not completely sure that it is 'the' Bible which God wrote through His prophets and apostles. And the 'room' eventually provides an excuse for man's arbitrary thinking to intervene in the interpretation of God's Word: not by the principles of the Word, but by man's judgment. The interpretation of the Bible, involving man's arbitrary judgment, is the same as distorting the original intention of God, the original Author of the Bible, and putting man's thoughts in place of God's Word. It results in the delivering of the word of man, not the Word of God. Then, the congregations eventually experience the absence of God's Word. This is not only a preacher's problem. Even when the preacher correctly interprets and properly preaches the Word according to the principles of the Bible, if the congregations are not convinced that the Word preached is 'the' Word that was written by God's inspiration and has been perfectly preserved without any error or mistake, they will not accept it as it is. The lack of trust in God's Word, delivered accurately and correctly, eventually provides an excuse for arbitrary and biased acceptance and application by the congregations themselves. It is not to correct their thoughts and opinions based on the inerrant and infallible Word of God, but rather to change the Word according to their thoughts and opinions. The arbitrary alteration of God's Word is, after all, nothing but just accepting their thoughts, not God's Word.

As such, confidence and trust in God's Word have an important effect on both the preacher and the congregations. This is very crucial for the inerrant and infallible Word of God, which is necessary and sufficient for man, to be communicated and accepted by them as God originally intended at His writing: positively and negatively as well. Confidence and trust in God's Word, inerrant and infallible, does not stop at the fact that the Bible was written by God's inspiration (Verbal Plenary Inspiration, 2 Tim 3:16). It must be accompanied by the fact that God, the original Author of the Bible, has preserved His written Word to this day (Verbal Plenary Preservation). It is because, if God's written Word has not been perfectly preserved by God Himself to this day, it is actually meaningless that He wrote it by His inspiration through the pen of human writers (Verbal Plenary Inspiration). When God gave His Word through 'writing' by His inspiration, His intention was to preserve and transmit it not only at the time of its writing but also to the distant future.[1,2,3] Moreover, the 'preservation' of the Word is the promise of God, the original Author of the Word. God promised to preserve His truth forever, without being bound by the limited time of man (Mt 5:18; 24:35; 1 Pet 1:23-25; Ps 12:6-7). Therefore, as Verbal Plenary Preservation of the Scriptures is secured according to God's promise, its Verbal Plenary Inspiration also has a significant meaning today as it was when the originals (autographs) were written. In other words, Verbal Plenary Inspiration, the principle of God's writing of the Bible, and its consistent on-going preservation, i.e. Verbal Plenary Preservation, are essential and indispensable elements of each other, in both their existence and function.

Most Bible-related problems today arise from denying or rejecting Verbal Plenary Preservation. The faction that denies Verbal Plenary Preservation admits Verbal Plenary Inspiration, but claims that Verbal Plenary Preservation is impossible or non-existent. Their denial or distrust of Verbal Plenary Preservation stems from how they view the process of preserving the Bible itself: not from a Word-based perspective, but from a human perspective. However, one thing they are mistaken is that the Subject who performs the preservation of the Bible is not man. Through His Word, God has already directly promised to preserve it by Himself, and it is clearly stated in the Bible: For instance, Jesus Christ said in Matthew 5:18, "For verily I say unto you, Till heaven and earth pass, one jot or one tittle shall in no wise pass from the law, till all be fulfilled." This is not a guarantee of man, but a confirmation by Jesus Christ, who is God Himself. Not only in the New Testament, but through David's mouth in Psalm 12:6-7, God specifies the preservation of His Word. Particularly David says in verse 7, "Thou shalt keep them, O LORD, thou shalt preserve them from this generation for ever." Here, "them" means "the words of the LORD" in the previous verse (verse 6), revealing that it is God Himself who is keeping the Word.[4] In this way, God had already promised through His Word that He would preserve it forever, and today He still continues to faithfully keep His promise. Therefore, the problem with Verbal Plenary Preservation is not from God; all the problems that arise from it come from the perspective of how a man views

---

[1] Lloyd L. Streeter, *Seventy-five Problems: with Central Baptist Seminary's Book - The Bible Version Debate* (Lasalle, IL: First Baptist Church of LaSalle, 2001), 126.

[2] Kent Brandenbug, ed., *Thou Shalt Keep Them: A Biblical Theology of the Perfect Preservation of Scripture* (El Sobrante, CA: Pillar & Ground Publishing, 2003), 65-68.

[3] G. John Rov, *Concealed from Christians for the Glory of God: The 1611 KJV - The King James Bible Authorized Version* (Morrisville, NC: Lulu Press, Inc., 2019), 35-37.

[4] The discussion of the conflict between the feminine Hebrew noun representing "words" and the masculine suffix "them" in Psalm 12:6-7 will be discussed in detail in a later chapter.

the Bible. In other words, all that matters concerning the preservation of the Bible is that of believing it as the Word that God wrote by His inspiration and still provides today as He has preserved it to the present day. And it eventually results in the matter of faith in God, the Subject who promises and keeps the preservation of the Word.

Purpose of the Research

As discussed above, God has perfectly preserved His Word, which He Himself wrote through men, according to His promise. God has preserved it through His chosen prophets and apostles, and through His faithful Church, which has been established by Jesus Christ Himself. And in the course of its preservation, the Word of God has been preserved to this day in the 'apographs,' which are the faithfully copied Scriptures, namely: the 'Masoretic' Old Testament Text written in Hebrew (and Aramaic in some parts), and the *'Textus Receptus'* - the New Testament Text in Greek. And all the believers in the churches today can still access the original words written by God's inspiration through these faithful traditional texts. Therefore, God is not responsible for the problems arising in connection with the perfect preservation of His written Word, the Bible: for He has faithfully and surely kept His own promise about His Word. Thus, the responsibility of all debates about the preservation of the Bible ultimately boils down to men. It has to do with man's view and attitude toward God's promise, which is still valid today through His written Word. Thus, this study is to examine human responsibility in relation to the perfect preservation of the Bible, God's written Word. There have been several studies dealing with Verbal Plenary Preservation in terms of God's promise. However, in the biblical refutation of the Preservation-related debates, few papers specifically address this issue in terms of human responsibility. And human responsibility for the preservation of the Bible must be reviewed focusing on the command of God, as the leading Subject of Verbal Plenary Preservation. It is God Himself who must preserve the Word, but in the process of preserving the Word as in the writing of it, God has used man as His instrument. Just as God used human writers to pen the words He inspired, He has made His faithful Church take part in the process of preserving His written words. Therefore, the Church, given the opportunity to participate in the process of preservation of the Word, must keep in mind and obey God's command for the God-written-and-preserved Word as well as His promise about it. This determines the Church's thoughts and attitudes toward God's Word; and, in the end, her thoughts and attitudes toward God Himself, the original Author of the Word.

This study aims to examine the issue of Verbal Plenary Preservation, especially focusing on God's 'command' for His completed written Word, which He has repeatedly emphasized in it. Like God's immutability, His Word also never changes (Ps 12:7; 1 Pet 1:25). Without stopping there, God severely and sternly forbids man from attempting to change the Word He completed. The most representative example of God's command regarding the prohibition of changing His Word is Revelation 22:18-19, the last chapter of the last book of the Bible. However, the same command is found in the very first book of the Bible: meaning that this command is consistently applied from the beginning to the end of the 66 books of the Bible. The writer of this study calls this consistent command of God, which strictly forbids any alteration by man, 'the Law of Inalterability,' focusing on human responsibility for Verbal Plenary Preservation. Since God is faithful and still keeps His promises also faithfully, He demands the same attitude from His Church. However, all the debates that have accumulated thus far in relation to Verbal Plenary Preservation have resulted from man's disobedience to God's commands related to it, 'the Law of Inalterability.' Therefore, in order to grasp the core of this matter and to accurately diagnose it, it is necessary to study what 'the Law of Inalterability' is. The primary purpose of this study is to examine the Scriptural texts related to how God commands 'the Law of Inalterability' from the beginning to the end of the Bible and to see how it relates to Verbal Plenary Preservation. Furthermore, the writer observes what practical phenomena appear in the process of preservation of the Word, due to disobedience to 'the Law of Inalterability.' In other words, an empirical analysis is conducted to compare the result of faithful obedience to 'the Law of Inalterability' with that of disobedience to it. To this end, this study contrasts the critical texts (Nestle-Aland 27th and 28th editions) with the *Textus Receptus*, specifically targeting the General Epistles. The *Textus Receptus* is the received New Testament Greek text that God has preserved through His faithful Church. Meanwhile, the Nestle-Aland editions based on the critical texts has been most widely used for the translation of modern versions. Therefore, the comparison between these two Greek texts can be a good observation which clearly shows the result of whether or not to obey God's command, 'the Law of Inalterability,' given to His Church that has been involved in the process of God's faithful preservation of His written Word. And since the controversies related to Verbal Plenary Preservation are mainly concentrated in the New Testament rather than the Old Testament, it is meaningful to compare the outcomes of obedience or disobedience to 'the Law of Inalterability' with the General Epistles. It is expected that this will be useful to discuss how the reactions of obedience or disobedience to 'the Law of Inalterability' that God commands throughout the whole Bible come out differently, and how they relate to the controversies over Verbal Plenary Preservation.

Methodology of the Research

'The Law of Inalterability' and Verbal Plenary Preservation are God's command for and promise of His Word. Therefore, in order to deal with the issue of 'the Law of Inalterability' with Verbal Plenary Preservation, its basis must be the Word of God itself. It is because God's Word is self-interpretive, and thus working as the best tool and commentary for its interpretation.[5] In other words, God's written Word, the Bible, is a necessary and sufficient standard for judging right and wrong and for making the correct diagnosis. Westminster Shorter Catechism Question No.2 answers the final authority of

---

[5] Robert E. Clayton, *All Scripture Advocate* (Maitland, FL; Xulon Press, 2003), 141. Clayton says, "All of Scripture provides us with the only standard of our faith and practice."

the Bible[6]: "The Word of God, which is contained in the Scriptures of the Old and New Testaments, is the only rule to direct us how we may glorify and enjoy him." And its Question No.3 states, "The Scriptures principally teach what man is to believe concerning God, and what duty God requires of man."[7] Therefore, there is no better material than the Bible itself in studying God's command of 'the Law of Inalterability.' It is based on the Bible, but other theological books and articles related to 'the Law of Inalterability' and Verbal Plenary Preservation are also used as references. And the *Textus Receptus* (Scrivener, 1908) is used for an empirical analysis related to 'the Law of Inalterability.' And as a control group for the *Textus Receptus*, Nestle-Aland Greek text, the 27th and the 28th (the most recent revised) editions, is also put together for an empirical analysis. Since the first edition of Nestle-Aland Greek text was published in 1898, it has been constantly revised. The 27th edition was published in 1993; and in 2008, Jack Moorman reported in his book that over 8,000 differences were found between it and the *Textus Receptus*.[8] But without stopping at the 27th edition, it was revised again. Accordingly, the 28th edition, the latest version of Nestle-Aland Greek text, was published in 2012, 21 years after the 27th edition was published. However, there has not yet been any book comparing the 27th and 28th editions of Nestle-Aland Greek text with the *Textus Receptus*.

The study proceeds as follows: In CHAPTER I, the doctrines of the Bible are explained first. 'The Law of Inalterability' is a command for God's Word. Therefore, before looking earnestly into 'the Law of Inalterability,' the core doctrines of the Bible, which is God's written Word and the basis of 'the Law of Inalterability,' must first be understood. Here, two core doctrines of the Bible are discussed: the principle of God's writing of the Bible (Verbal Plenary Inspiration) and His promise on its preservation (Verbal Plenary Preservation). CHAPTER II discusses the subject of this study – 'the Law of Inalterability.' After first examining the features of the truth, Bible-based textual studies of 'the Law of Inalterability' are conducted. In addition, the link between 'the Law of Inalterability' and Verbal Plenary Preservation is examined, and further, some practical issues related to the two are also dealt with. In CHAPTER III, an empirical analysis is conducted to observe the actual phenomena according to 'the Law of Inalterability' and people's reaction toward that command (obedience or disobedience). For empirical analysis, a comparative analysis is performed between the critical texts (Nestle-Aland 27th and 28th editions) and the traditional/received text (*Textus Receptus*), focusing on the General Epistles of the New Testament. Then, based on the results of the comparative analysis between the two texts shown in the General Epistles, observations with interpretations are made on where the differences come from. This is to find out in which part of the General Epistles of the critical texts arbitrary alterations were attempted

---

[6] Shorter Catechism of the Assembly of Divines, "WESTMINSTER SHORTER CATECHISM: WITH PROOF TEXT," A Puritan's Mind, accessed on December 23, 2019, http://www.reformed.org/documents/wsc/index.html?_top=http://www.reformed.org/documents/WSC.html.

[7] Shorter Catechism of the Assembly of Divines, *ibid.*

[8] Jack Moorman, *8,000 Differences Between the N.T. Greek Words of the King James Bible and the Modern Versions* (London, England: The Old Paths Publications, Inc., 2008).

due to disobedience to 'the Law of Inalterability.' Then, it is diagnosed whether obedience or disobedience to 'the Law of Inalterability' affects the attitudes and outcomes of those who have been participating in the preservation process of the Word of God. Finally, from the results of all reviews and analysis of this study, a comprehensive conclusion regarding 'the Law of Inalterability' is drawn.

CHAPTER I. THE DOCTRINE OF THE BIBLE: VERBAL PLENARY INSPIRATION AND VERBAL PLENARY PRESERVATION

1.1 Verbal Plenary Inspiration: God's Principle
1.1.1 Biblical Definition of Verbal Plenary Inspiration

The primary Author of the Bible is God Himself. God used the hands of the human writers who were chosen by Him according to His holy will to pen the Scriptures, but everything written in the Bible is undoubtedly the Word of God coming out of Himself. First, the Bible consistently describes that all the written words are spoken directly from the mouth of God. Proverbs 2:6 said, "For the LORD giveth wisdom: out of his mouth cometh knowledge and understanding." Also, the prophet Isaiah had proclaimed many times that every word he spoke was God's own word from His mouth, and it must be fulfilled (Isa 45:23; 48:3; 55:11). The Hebrew preposition "מִן" that is used here basically means 'from' or 'out of,' but also implies 'source or origin.'[9] Deuteronomy 8:3 is what God said was declared to the Israelites through Moses and also recorded ("… man doth not live by bread only, but by every word that proceedeth out of the mouth of the LORD doth man live"). Here, the Hebrew word מוֹצָא for "proceedeth" has its root in יָצָא, which means 'going out/forth' or 'utterance.'[10] All these records show that the Utterer of all the words of the Bible is God Himself. John W. Burgon declares this through the following statement. This declaration concisely but clearly shows the faith in God's perfect and pure Word and the higher view of the Bible:

> The Bible is none other than <u>the voice</u> of Him that sitteth upon the throne! Every book of it, every chapter of it, every verse of it, every word of it, every syllable of it, every letter of it, is <u>the direct utterance</u> of the Most High! The Bible is none other than <u>the Word</u> of God: not some part of it more, some part of it less; but all alike <u>the utterance</u> of Him that sitteth upon the throne; faultless, unerring, supreme![11]
>
> (emphasis added)

In addition, the Bible testifies that God is the direct Writer of His Word. Exodus 20:1-17 speaks of a scene where God gave the Israelites the Ten Commandments through Moses. On Mount Sinai, God first gave His words onto the two tablets that were made by God Himself and then given to Moses (Exod 31:18, 32:16). Here, the important thing is that God wrote them all by His own hand ("two tables of testimony, tables of stone, written with the finger of God," Exod 31:18). This principle remained consistent even when God gave the very same words a second time after Moses broke the first stone

---

[9] Ronald J. Williams, *Williams' Hebrew Syntax*, 3rd ed. (Toronto, Canada: University of Toronto Press, 2007), 122-123.

[10] F. Brown, S. Driver, and C. Briggs, *The Brown-Driver-Briggs Hebrew and English Lexicon* (Peabody: Hendrickson Publishers, 1996), 425.

[11] "Dean Burgon Oath," Far Eastern Bible College, accessed on February 06, 2020, https://www.febc.edu.sg/v15/article/def_the_dean_burgon_oath.

tablets due to the golden calf incident ("I will write upon these tables the words that were in the first tables, which thou brakest," Exod 34:1b). The point here is "I will write upon these tables": just like the first ones, God once again wrote the very same words by His own hand and gave it to Moses. This is recorded once more in the recollection of Moses in the Book of Deuteronomy (Deut 9:9-21).

All the written words of God, the Bible, were directly spoken by God Himself as the original Author, but in the process of 'writing' the Bible, He used human writers that He specifically chose. However, this does not mean that God intended to depend on their human power. They, their individual competencies, were only chosen by God to be used as humble instruments for the original writing of God's Word. God does not need human power at all to accomplish His work, but rather man absolutely needs God's almighty power.[12] Since the Bible is the very Word of God, every letter written by human writers is very important and vital. However, since it was impossible to pen the Word of God without any mistakes by their own means, it was necessary for human writers to ask for the help of the Holy Spirit. Therefore, all human writers chosen by God's special providence completely had to rely on the special cares of the Holy Spirit to do their writing works of His inspired Word. The help of the Holy Spirit is absolutely essential to those human writers because the Holy Spirit is none other than "the Spirit of truth" (Jn 14:17; 15:26; 16:13). Thus, the Holy Spirit works for and with the Word of God, the truth. In addition to 2 Timothy 3:16, there are more evidences in the Bible that the Holy Spirit is with God's Word and works for it.

In the New Testament. First, John 15:26 says: "But when the Comforter is come, whom I will send unto you from the Father, even the Spirit of truth, which proceedeth from the Father, he shall testify of me." Here, "Comforter" is another name for the Holy Spirit, whose role is to testify and teach about Jesus Christ, the living Word, and His words (Jn 14:26). The Apostle John testifies in another epistle that the One who testifies of Jesus Christ is none other than the Spirit of truth (1 Jn 5:6-7). Also, the fact that the early church members experienced 'speaking in tongues'[13] at the scene where the Holy Spirit descended, as at the Pentecostal event as described in the Acts of the Apostles, is thoroughly related to the speaking, hearing, and understanding of the Word of truth ("as the Spirit gave them utterance," Acts 2:4; "the Holy Ghost fell on all them which heard the word," Acts 10:44; emphasis added). In this way, the Word of God and the Holy Spirit are inseparable. In particular, Acts 2:4 indicates that the Holy Spirit directly gave what

---

[12] In Exodus 3:14, God defines Himself as "I AM THAT I AM." God is not created by someone like all things in this world: He is self-existent. Therefore, God is already the perfect Being Himself, without any need to rely on anything. Rather, human beings are fragile beings that cannot exist without God.

[13] 'Speaking in tongue' was to prove the authenticity of the words spoken by the Apostles, along with other miracles God had allowed. But after the completion of God's written Word, the Bible, all of them were completely stopped. 1 Corinthians 13:8-10 is the proof text for this fact. Especially in one of the phrases of 1 Corinthians 13:8, "whether there be tongues, they shall cease," the Greek verb for "shall cease" here is written in the future middle deponent, indicating that 'speaking in tongue' was stopped 'by itself' with the completion of the written Word (1 Cor 13:10; τὸ τέλειον as a 'neuter' noun).

the Apostles would say.[14] In other words, it means that the actual Speaker is the Holy Spirit Himself, even though He used the Apostles' mouth.

In the Old Testament. Further evidences are observed from the Old Testament where the Holy Spirit spoke the Word of God. 2 Samuel 23:2 says, "The Spirit of the LORD spake by me, and his word was in my tongue." David's words imply that he was used as a prophet, just as a tool to deliver the word of the Lord, not his own word. And in the expression "his word," David testifies that the Holy Spirit, who was dwelling in him, placed the word of the Lord in his mouth, which he should deliver. Isaiah 59:21b says, "My spirit that is upon thee, and my words which I have put in thy mouth." Here, "My" stands for "the LORD," showing that God, who came as Redeemer[15] to His people with the presence of the Holy Spirit, put His words ("my words") into the mouth of the prophet Isaiah. Therefore, the Old Testament also testifies that the Word of God and the Holy Spirit are inseparable.

<u>Word Study of Inspiration: 2 Timothy 3:16</u>

God also left a record in the Bible about how He wrote His Word. Verbal Plenary Inspiration is the principle by which God wrote His Word, and the clear fact that the Bible was written by the inspiration of the Holy Spirit was recorded in the Greek original text and King James Version for 2 Timothy 3:16 respectively as below:

πᾶσα γραφὴ <u>θεόπνευστος</u> καὶ ὠφέλιμος πρὸς διδασκαλίαν, πρὸς ἔλεγχον, πρὸς ἐπανόρθωσιν, πρὸς παιδείαν τὴν ἐν δικαιοσύνῃ [*Textus Receptus*]
All scripture is given <u>by inspiration of God</u>, and is profitable for doctrine, for reproof, for correction, for instruction in righteousness [King James Version]
(Emphasis added)

The word "inspiration of God" in the Greek text is θεόπνευστος, which is from two different compounds: θεός and πνέω. Thayer's lexicon defines this word as "inspired by God," which in particular refers to "the contents of Scripture" in combination with "scripture" (γραφὴ). Here, θεός is a noun meaning 'God' and πνέω is a verb meaning 'to breathe' or 'to blow.'[16] These two words are combined to mean 'God-breathed.' This word signifies Divine inspiration, and is a New Testament *hapax legomenon*, used only once in 2 Timothy 3:16.

The verses that express God's Word in relation to His 'breath' can also be found in the Old Testament. Among them, Psalm 33:6 praises God's power of creation made through His words: "By the word of the LORD were the heavens made; and all the host of them by the breath of his mouth." What is interesting here is that 'synonymous

---

[14] Who the "them" in Acts 2:3 is must be interpreted according to the context. In the later part of Acts 1, the remaining eleven apostles selected Matthias as a new apostle for the vacant seat of Judas Iscariot. Immediately thereafter, Acts 2:1 puts "And" (Καὶ) at its very beginning, indicating that it is a continuation of the narrative from the last part of Acts 1. In this context, it can be understood that "they" in Acts 2:1 (also in 2:4) are 'the' apostles, and also "them" in 2:3.

[15] C.F. Keil and F. Delitzsch, *Commentary on the Old Testament* (New Zealand: Titus Books, 2014), 7069.

[16] Joseph H. Thayer, *Thayer's Greek-English Lexicon of the New Testament* (Grand Rapids, Michigan: Baker Book House, 1977), 287-288, 524.

parallelism' is used, in which "by the word of the LORD" is expressed in parallel with "by the breath of his mouth." The highlight here is "breath." In the Hebrew text for the same verse, רוּחַ was used, followed by "his mouth" (פִּיו), showing that "breath" is "God's breath." The Septuagint (LXX) adopted the Greek word πνευματι for "breath" in the same passage. In the same vein, Zechariah 7:12 writes that the words transmitted through the mouth of the prophets are "the words which the LORD of hosts hath sent in his spirit." Here, the Hebrew equivalent of "in his spirt" is בְּרוּחוֹ, which is the same context as רוּחַ used earlier in Psalm 33:6.[17] רוּחַ as used herein all means "spirit" or "breath," and has the same meaning as πνέω used in 2 Timothy 3:16. Another word derived from πνέω is πνεῦμα, which has the meaning of 'breath' in the same context as πνέω. Also, in addition to 'spirit' in the general sense, πνεῦμα stands for 'the Holy Spirit,' especially in relation to God.[18] Robbie F. Castleman cites the words of William D. Mounce in his book, defining the "inspired" of 2 Timothy 3:16 as "from the mouth of God." He also describes "the Spirit" as "the very breath of God."[19] This is in line with "by the breath of his mouth" of Psalm 33:6, showing that 'the breath of God' is used interchangeably with 'the Spirit of God' as the same meaning. Therefore, as can be seen from all these facts, 'God-breathed' and 'the Holy Spirit' are mutually inseparable. That is why 'the Word of God' and 'the breath of God (from His mouth)' are connected in the Old Testament as well as in the New Testament, which means 'the Spirit of God.'

On the other hand, there is one more important note in 2 Timothy 3:16, that the object to which is pointed by θεόπνευστος is nothing but γραφὴ itself. In πᾶσα γραφὴ θεόπνευστος, πᾶσα γραφὴ as the subject is modified by θεόπνευστος. Thus, its Greek scripture shows that when God used the human writers as His instruments to pen His words, He "breathed" through the Holy Spirit to the product of their writing works (i.e. the Word of God itself), not to the writers themselves. In other words, θεόπνευστος or "God-breathed" in 2 Timothy 3:16 is a tangible expression that the process of writing the Word of God was completely guided by the Holy Spirit; Not only that, θεόπνευστος is a word revealing that 'all words' in the Bible are perfectly penned according to God's intended will without any error or mistake, through the thorough lead and guidance of the Holy Spirit, even though God used each human writer's personality, thoughts, or judgments. The King James Version translated θεόπνευστος as "inspiration," and Richard A. Muller, integrating "God-breathed" and "inspired," defines "the human authors of Scripture as acted upon by the Spirit in their work of writing and the character of the resulting written text as Word of God."[20] That is to say, θεόπνευστος is the wording to reveal the fact that the Author of the written Word, the entirety of the Scriptures, is none other than God Himself.

---

[17] Septuagint (LXX) also adopted πνευματι the same as in Psalm 33:6.

[18] Thayer, *Thayer's Greek-English Lexicon of the New Testament*, 520-523.

[19] Robbie F. Castleman, *Interpreting the God-Breathed Word: How to Read and Study the Bible* (Grand Rapid, MI: Baker Academic, 2018), 14.

[20] Richard A. Muller, *Dictionary of Latin and Greek Theological Terms* (Grand Rapid, MI: Baker Book House, 1985), 304.

1.1.2 Literature Review on Verbal Plenary Inspiration

Charles C. Ryrie defines 'inspiration' as follows: "God's superintendence of the human authors so that, using their own individual personalities, they composed and recorded without error His revelation to man in the words of the original autographs." Along with this definition, he also introduces various mistaken views about 'inspiration' into seven categories.[21] Each of these views has some elements that are against the true principles of writing the Bible, which God says in 2 Timothy 3:16:

First, 'natural inspiration': In this view, the human writers of the Bible are considered as prodigious geniuses like any other geniuses in history. This is a view that denies God's supernatural providence and treats the Bible just as the inspired writings of those geniuses in general meaning. Therefore, the term 'inspiration' here means something completely different from that of 2 Timothy 3:16.

Second, 'mystical inspiration': This is also called 'the illumination view of inspiration,' as a view that treats the human writers of the Bible as the "Spirit-filled and guided" Christians, just like ordinary believers. Thus, this view asserts that even ordinary "Spirit-filled Christians" can write the Bible, and that the writers of the Bible were only inspired to a greater extent than those ordinary ones. In this view, it is denied that God chose those human writers in His special providence for the penning of His written Word.

Third, 'inspiration as dictation': This view is that God allowed His human writers only to passively write down His words, completely ignoring the characteristics and traits of each writer. However, if any brief review of the Hebrew or Greek Scriptures is made, this view is immediately refuted, because God used writer-specific characteristics and traits, including their writing styles.

Fourth, 'partial inspiration': This is the view that only certain parts of the Bible were supernaturally inspired. This is in line with the modernistic view of the textual critics like Westcott and Hort about the Bible. By deliberately altering 2 Timothy 3:16 in the translation of the Revised Version, they denied God's Word that the entire Bible was inspired.[22]

Fifth, 'conceptual inspiration': In this view, it is argued that the concepts, not the words of the Bible, were inspired. This view denies the complete accuracy of all the words written in the Bible, and thus stands against the Bible's inerrancy and infallibility.

Sixth, 'the Bible as a witness': This view is of the neoorthodoxy or the Barthian, accepting the liberal views of the Bible. They claim that the Bible 'becomes' the Word of God. In other words, they admit that Christ is primarily the Word, but the Bible, the written Word, is considered just as a product of fallible writers, with full of errors. Therefore, in this view, it is argued that the Bible becomes the Word of God as a witness to Christ, only when it is preached to the people and bring about faith in Christ.[23]

---

[21] Charles C. Ryrie, *A Survey of Bible Doctrine* (Chicago: Moody Publishers, 1972), 28-29.

[22] Jeffrey Khoo, *Kept Pure in All Ages* (Singapore: Far Eastern Bible College Press, 2001), 143-144.

[23] Bruce K. Waltke, *An Old Testament Theology: An Exegetical, Canonical, and Thematic Approach* (Grand Rapids, Michigan: Zondervan Academic, 2007), 75.

Seventh, 'purposeful inspiration': This is an over-focus on the "doctrinal integrity" of the Bible, with the view that there is no real error or difference in contents unless there is a problem in the core doctrine, which God intends to reveal through the Bible (especially the doctrine of salvation through Jesus Christ). Thus, paradoxically, this view basically presupposes that the Bible contains errors, but nevertheless asserts that if the doctrine is revealed, it has accomplished God's purpose through the Bible. Thus, despite being more conservative than the Barthians, it is the same in denying the inerrancy and infallibility of the whole Bible (as the entirety of the Bible).

However, these views do not accept the principle of writing the Bible that God has already said, but incorporates human thoughts and interpretations into it. Verbal Plenary Inspiration is not a new doctrine, but the principle that God has already clearly revealed through His written Word, the Bible. Here, all the dictionary definitions of 'verbal' are related to 'words' themselves, having the meanings "of, relating to, or consisting of words" or "of, relating to, or involving words rather than meaning or substance."[24] Thus, 'verbal' used in the doctrine of Verbal Plenary Inspiration refers to all the words themselves written in the Bible; 'Plenary' is "complete in every respect: absolute, unqualified,"[25] being used to speak the entire Bible. Thus, Verbal Plenary Inspiration means that every word in the Bible and the Bible itself as a whole was inspired by God, based on Matthew 5:18 ("one jot or one tittle") and 2 Timothy 3:16.[26] Also, Verbal Plenary Inspiration is the principle that goes for the original languages (the Old Testament in Hebrew and Aramaic, the New Testament in Greek) in which God wrote His Word, not the translated versions. Paché defines Verbal Plenary Inspiration as meaning that, throughout the Bible, the Holy Spirit guided even the expressions the human writers used without the effacement of their own personalities in the composition of the original manuscripts. Since the words are inseparable with the messages intended to be communicated through them, the Divine revelations God wants to communicate through the Bible also have an inseparable relationship with the languages used for writing the Bible. Therefore, since the entire Scripture is composed of the God-breathed words, it eventually means the inspiration of the Scripture itself.[27] H. D. Williams reflects all of these contexts and exegetically defines 'inspiration' in his book as follows: "Inspiration is the miracle whereby the Words of Scripture in Hebrew, Aramaic and Greek were God-breathed and once delivered using holy men of God and their vocabulary, who perfectly recorded them once as they were moved along by the Holy Spirit in such a way that all the Words written are infallible and inerrant in the sixty-six books of the canon of Scripture."[28] Therefore, Verbal Plenary Inspiration is God's

---

[24] "Verbal," Merriam-Webster, accessed on May 07, 2020, https://www.merriam-webster.com/dictionary/verbal.

[25] "Plenary," Merriam-Webster, accessed on May 07, 2020, https://www.merriam-webster.com/dictionary/plenary.

[26] George Skariah, "The Biblical Doctrine of the Perfect Preservation of the Holy Scriptures" (PhD diss., Far Eastern Bible College Press, 2005), 2.

[27] René Paché, *The Inspiration and Authority of Scripture* (Chicago: Moody Press, 1969), 71-79.

[28] H. D. Williams, *The Miracle of Biblical Inspiration* (Cleveland, Georgia: The Old Paths Publications Inc., 2009), 27.

principle that contains the necessary validity of the inerrancy and infallibility of the Bible. Many faithful church fathers, reformers and even modern writers have also stuck to the doctrine of the inerrancy of the Scripture. Shortly after the Apostolic age, well-known church fathers such as Clement, Irenaeus, and Augustine affirmed the Scriptural inerrancy without any doubt. Calvin, along with Luther, also affirmed the infallibility of the Scripture, saying, "the apostles were the certain and authentic scribes of the Holy Spirit, and therefore their writings are to be received as the oracles of God." And Wesley also had the high view of the inspiration of the Bible, so he never allowed the idea that the Bible was errant. Meanwhile, Edward J. Young, a leading modern writer and reformed scholar, also wrote a statement enunciating the inerrancy of the Bible in 1957 when he was serving at the Westminster Theological Seminary. As such, their reliable and express testimonies of the inerrancy and infallibility of the Scripture show that this important fact and core doctrine can only be trusted by the Holy Spirit's internal testimony in the mind of genuine believers.[29] Thus, the principle of the written Word inspired by the Holy Spirit, which God clearly revealed through His Word, and of course the inerrancy and infallibility of the Scripture following that principle, are the important doctrines requiring genuine faith and testimony of the Holy Spirit.

However, the core doctrine of Verbal Plenary Inspiration (the Bible as the God-breathed written Word) has faced oppositions and attacks from those who deny it. The representative deniers are the liberals or the modernists. Machen points to the unbelief of the modern liberals in the doctrine of plenary inspiration. According to Machen, the liberals also deny the doctrine of inerrancy and infallibility of the Bible as well as that of plenary inspiration, because of their preconception that the Holy Spirit was "mechanically dictating" to the human writers of the Bible, and their way of thinking that puts more emphasis on their experiences than the Word itself. Even the liberal theologians show a "mechanical response," advocating the "mechanical" theory, but rejecting the review of the existence of errors. However, Machen again points out that this phenomenon is observed not only in the liberal camp, but also in many other Christian camps. The modern liberals even dismiss the value of the Bible as a reliable ordinary book, and more than that, even the Gospels of Christ that is the only part accepted by them are selectively mangled by the textual criticism they ardently advocate. Because of this kind of low view and dismissal of the Bible (with abysmal skepticism), they bring down even Christ, who is the real Authority of truth proclaimed through the Bible, to the level of general morality.[30] Representative liberal theologians include Briggs and Thayer, who were active in the late 19th and early 20th centuries. They reacted against Warfield and Hodge, who were the representative Old Princeton theologians and defended the "biblical inspiration." Briggs was a devotee of higher criticism, relying on human reason to deny God's transcendental history. In advocating the inspiration confined to the

---

[29] Stewart Custer, *Does Inspiration Demand Inerrancy? A Study of the Biblical Doctrine of Inspiration in the Light of Inerrancy* (Nutley, New Jersey: the Craig Press, 1968), 63-67.

[30] J. Gresham Machen, *Christianity and Liberalism* (Grand Rapids, Michigan: WM. B. Eerdmans Publishing Company, 1923), 69-79.

spiritual message in the Bible, he rejected the doctrine of verbal inspiration and inerrancy as unfounded. What's worse, Thayer of Harvard University supported Briggs' claim who advocated the scientific worldview as well as higher criticism as a modernist. Briggs and Thayer were representative liberals who insisted on changing the understanding of Christianity and biblical authority based on modern thoughts and higher criticism. However, on their claim, Warfield proved that this important core doctrine, biblical inspiration and inerrancy, has been continuously affirmed by the Westminster Standards, as well as by Calvin, and even by Augustine, the representative first Church father.[31]

1.2 Verbal Plenary Preservation: God's Promise
1.2.1 Biblical Definition of Verbal Plenary Preservation

Another important doctrine of the Bible is Verbal Plenary Preservation of the Scriptures. Verbal Plenary Preservation means God's 'special providential preservation of the Scriptures,' which is distinct from His general providence. If God's general or ordinary providence (*providentia ordinaria*) is the way God rules and preserves this world through the instrumentality of secondary causes in accordance with the natural laws, His special or extraordinary providence (*providentia extraordinaria*) means his special acts or miracles, going beyond the normal possibilities inherent in secondary causality.[32] In other words, Verbal Plenary Preservation means that God performed 'special acts': He 'inspired' His own words at the penning of human writers and 'has preserved' them continuously. The Westminster Confession of Faith Chapter 1.8 describes God's special providential preservation of the Scripture as "by his singular care and providence, kept pure in all ages." And, in addition, it is to say that the Old and New Testaments were written and have preserved to this day by God's direct intervention, in Hebrew and in Greek, respectively.[33] Since the original texts (autographs) that God wrote through human writers no longer remain, He has preserved His Word through the exact and identical copies (apographs) of the original texts (autographs).[34]

God has already promised in many places in the Bible the preservation of His Word. The most representative proof text for Verbal Plenary Preservation is Matthew 5:18, in which Jesus Christ declared that until the fulfillment of all His words, the Word of God, even any smallest thing, would never be damaged: "For verily I say unto you, Till heaven and earth pass, one jot or one tittle shall in no wise pass from the law, till all be fulfilled." In Matthew 24:35, in the same context, He said that His words will never

---

[31] Matthew Barrett, *God's Word Alone: The Authority of Scripture*, ePub ed. (Grand Rapids, Michigan: Zondervan, 2016), 91-93.

[32] Muller, *Dictionary of Latin and Greek Theological Terms*, 252.

[33] "Westminster Confession of Faith Chapter 1: Of the Holy Scripture - no.8," Bible Presbyterian Church General Synod, accessed on March 29, 2020, https://bpc.org/?page_id=542. In other words, Verbal Plenary Preservation states that God wrote the Old and New testaments both by His direct inspiration and has preserved them in Hebrew for the Old Testament, the language of Israel who are the people chosen according to God's special providence, and in Greek for the New Testament, the common language at the time when the New Testament was written.

[34] Discussions related to the manuscripts of the Scripture will be covered in more detail later in this chapter.

go away but be preserved: "Heaven and earth shall pass away, but my words shall not pass away." Also, through the Apostle Peter, God says that all things in this world will wither and disappear, but His words will last forever (1 Pet 1:24-25). And in Psalm 12:6-7, the psalmist praises the pure words of God that will be preserved forever: "The words of the LORD are pure words: as silver tried in a furnace of earth, purified seven times. Thou shalt keep them, O LORD, thou shalt preserve them from this generation for ever."

<u>Word Study of Preservation: Matthew 5:18</u>

Verbal Plenary Preservation already connotes its meaning within the definition of the term itself. First, the dictionary definition of 'verbal' is "consisting of or in the form of words" or "expressed in spoken words."[35] In other words, 'verbal' refers to "words," and in relation to the preservation of the Bible, it refers to God's written Word itself. "Plenary" means "full, complete" or "entire," meaning the entirety of the Bible from beginning to end. Thus, when these two words are combined with "preservation," Verbal Plenary Preservation is to say that God preserves all the words of the Bible, which He wrote as the original Author. Along with God's promises of preservation described in the Bible (Mt 5:18; 24:35; Ps 12:6-7; 1 Pet 1:25), Verbal Plenary Preservation can be defined in more detail as follows:

> The whole of Scripture with all its words even to the jot and tittle is perfectly preserved by God without any loss of the original words, prophecies, promises, commandments, doctrines, and truths, not only in the words of salvation, but also the words of history, geography and science. Every book, every chapter, every verse, every word, every syllable, every letter is infallibly preserved by the Lord Himself to the last iota.[36]

In Matthew 5:18, God says through the Greek New Testament (*Textus Receptus*) as follows: ἀμὴν γὰρ λέγω ὑμῖν, ἕως ἂν παρέλθῃ ὁ οὐρανὸς καὶ ἡ γῆ, ἰῶτα ἓν ἢ μία κεραία οὐ μὴ παρέλθῃ ἀπὸ τοῦ νόμου ἕως ἂν πάντα γένηται. Here, ἰῶτα is "jot," which is the smallest of the Hebrew letters, the "yohd" (ˈ); κεραία or "tittle" is also a very tiny extension among the Hebrew letters.[37] That is to say, "jot" and "tittle" are both expressions used to symbolize the smallest part of the Hebrew language system.[38, 39] Therefore, now God is saying that even the smallest part in the Bible He wrote will never disappear. Also, in the original Hebrew Scripture, νόμου (from νόμος meaning "law") represents "the Torah" or "Five Books of Moses (Pentateuch)" in a broad sense,

---

[35] "Verbal," Dictionary.com, accessed on March 29, 2020, https://www.dictionary.com/browse/verbal.

[36] "Definition of Verbal Plenary Preservation (VPP)," Far Eastern Bible College, accessed on March 29, 2020, https://www.febc.edu.sg/v15/article/verbal_plenary_preservation.

[37] John MacArthur, *The MacArthur New Testament Commentary* (Nashville, Tennessee: Thomas Nelson Publishers, 2007), 40.

[38] "ἰῶτα/Matthew 5:18," *Textus Receptus* Bibles, accessed on March 29, 2020, http://www.textusreceptusbibles.com/Strongs/40005018/G2503.

[39] "κεραία/Matthew 5:18," *Textus Receptus* Bibles, accessed on March 29, 2020, http://www.textusreceptusbibles.com/Strongs/40005018/G2762.

sometimes referring to the entire Old Testament.[40] Not only that, in verse 17 immediately preceding, Jesus Christ said, "Think not that I am come to destroy the law, or the prophets: I am not come to destroy, but to fulfil." Here, "the law, or the prophets" refers to the entire Old Testament. Then, He referred to νόμου in verse 18. Therefore, when considering not only the meaning of the Greek word itself, but also the contexts of verses 17 and 18 together, νόμου refers to the entire Old Testament, not part of it.[41] During the earthly life of Jesus Christ, only the Old Testament was the entire Bible of the Israelites, because the New Testament was not yet written. Thus, here Jesus Christ was affirming "the utter inerrancy and absolute authority of the OT as the Word of God" through this expression referring to the Old Testament.[42] Lastly, the aorist subjunctive (παρέλθη) is used together with οὐ μὴ as the "emphatic negative future,"[43] to emphasize that this will never happen ('shall never'). Putting all these together, Jesus Christ affirms that all of His written words will be preserved intact and untouched until every single word is fulfilled. This is a certain promise of the preservation of the Word made by Jesus Christ, who is God Himself and the living Word.

A similar remark is recorded in Matthew 24:35, where it is even expressed as "Heaven and earth shall pass away." This is one step further from the expression of "Till heaven and earth pass" mentioned in Matthew 5:18. Also, this verse directly refers to the Word of God as λόγοι. And in the Greek scripture of this verse, οὐ μὴ and the aorist subjunctive are used together in the same way as in Matthew 5:18. Hence, Matthew 24:35 also emphasizes that even if heaven and earth are gone, the Word of the Lord will never be lost but preserved.

1 Peter 1:24-25 further explains what "the word," which will never go away, is. ῥῆμα used in verse 25 means "utterance," and in the second half of the same verse, it is explained in detail that ῥῆμα is none other than "the gospel." From the very first time, as soon as the fall of man shortly after creation, God had already proclaimed this message of the Gospel by Himself (Gen 3:15; the first Gospel, *protevangelium*[44]), and it continued until the first coming of Jesus Christ. In addition, the New Testament is to testify of the earthly ministry of Jesus Christ, who already came, especially of His redemptive work He had accomplished; and to prophesy His return to come. Therefore, since the entire Bible from the Old Testament to the New Testament delivers the message of the Gospel, "the gospel" mentioned in verse 25 can be regarded as the entirety of the Word, the Bible, in a broad sense. Although this very Word had been preached to people through the mouths of prophets and apostles, it clearly shows that its direct Speaker is none other than

---

[40] "νόμος/Matthew 5:18," *Textus Receptus* Bibles, accessed on March 29, http://www.textusreceptusbibles.com/Strongs/40005018/G3551.

[41] R. C. H. Lenski, *The Interpretation of St. Matthew's Gospel* (Minneapolis, Minnesota: Augsburg Publishing House, 1943), 208-209.

[42] MacArthur, ibid.

[43] J. W. Wenham, *The Elements of New Testament Greek* (Cambridge, UK: Cambridge University Press, 1965), 163.

[44] E. W. Hengstenberg, *Christology of the Old Testament* (Grand Rapids, Michigan: Kregel Publications, 1970), 13-24.

"the Lord" Himself (Κυρίου as the 'ablative of source'). And it is also proclaimed through the Apostle Peter that "the word of the LORD" is eternal (εἰς τὸν αἰῶνα).

<u>Syntactical Argument on Preservation: Psalm 12:6-7</u>

Psalm 12:6-7 is one of the proof texts for Verbal Plenary Preservation: "The words of the LORD are pure words: as silver tried in a furnace of earth, purified seven times. Thou shalt keep them, O LORD, thou shalt preserve them from this generation for ever." The debate related to this scriptural text starts from the question of who "them" in verse 7 is pointing to. The fact that this is the subject of a heated debate can also be observed from the modern versions with the various different translations of this same verse (Ps 12:7):[45]

King James Version	"Thou shalt keep <u>them</u>, O LORD, thou shalt preserve <u>them</u> from this generation for ever"
New American Standard Bible	"You, O Lord, will keep <u>them</u>; You will preserve <u>him</u> from this generation forever"
New International Version	"You, Lord, will keep <u>the needy</u> safe and will protect <u>us</u> forever from the wicked"
New Living Translation	"Therefore, Lord, we know you will protect <u>the oppressed</u>, preserving <u>them</u> forever from this lying generation"
Revised Standard Version	"Do thou, O Lord, protect <u>us</u>, guard <u>us</u> ever from this generation"

(<u>emphasis added</u>)

When considering these translations, the modern versions other than the King James Version interpret "them" as referring to the preservation of people rather than that of the Word. Thus, the supportive role of this verse for Verbal Plenary Preservation can be confirmed when the object of "them" is accurately identified in the original Hebrew Scriptures.

This debate is about how to understand the two pronominal suffixes used for תִּשְׁמְרֵם תִּצְּרֶנּוּ of verse 7 in the Hebrew Scripture.[46] First, שָׁמַר, the root word of תִּשְׁמְרֵם, was used 468 times in the 440 verses of the Old Testament. As in Psalm 12:7, it was most commonly used in the Qal stem to mean "keep," followed by "observe," "heed," or "preserve" in frequency. The root word of the second word תִּצְּרֶנּוּ is נָצַר, which is used a total of 63 times in the Old Testament. This verb also takes the Qal stem, which is most often used to mean "keep," followed by "preserve." The controversial part of these two verbs is the pronominal suffixes attached to the end of each verb. תִּשְׁמְרֵם takes the suffix ם of the third person masculine plural form, and תִּצְּרֶנּוּ takes the suffix נּוּ with the energetic nun, which can be interpreted as either the third person masculine singular or the first person plural. However, the Hebrew noun for "words" in verse 7 is either אֲמָרוֹת or אִמֲרֹת,

---

[45] "Psalm 12:7," Bible Gateway, accessed on March 30, 2020, https://www.biblegateway.com.
[46] It is verse 8 in the Hebrew Scripture.

both of which are in feminine plural form. Here, the issue of the gender or number mismatch emerges.

First, the discrepancy between ם in תִּשְׁמְרֵם and וֹת in אִמְרוֹת or אֲמָרוֹת can be explained by the exception of the principle of gender agreement in the Hebrew Scriptures. Sometimes the distinction between masculine and feminine in the Hebrew Scriptures is ambiguous or weakens.[47] This is especially observed in the plural form, and the most representative example is the plural form of the masculine noun אָב (father) - אָבוֹת (fathers). Also, as in Job 1:14, the suffix of the masculine plural form is sometimes used for the female plural antecedent.[48] Therefore, the gender mismatch problem between ם and וֹת can be interpreted in this context. Meanwhile, נּוּ in תִּצְּרֶנּוּ should be reviewed in other aspects. This suffix נּוּ with the energetic nun has two possibilities: the first-person plural or the third-person masculine singular. Here, the plural form exists only in the first person, and the interesting thing is that this first-person plural form can be applied to all other plural forms. That means נּוּ can be interpreted as the third person masculine plural rather than the first-person plural. However, it is impossible to interpret נּוּ as the suffix in the general third person masculine singular form. It is because the subject אַתָּה refers to the immediately following יְהוָה, if it is an object in the general third-person masculine singular, it becomes the meaning of "the LORD will keep Himself." This is not logically tenable. However, when the energetic nun is used with a verb, it serves the purpose of giving greater emphasis on the verb.[49] For this purpose, especially in the sense of "each one (of them)," it is used to highlight each belonging to a particular group. And the gender mismatch problem between נּוּ and וֹת can be interpreted in the same context as the problem between ם and וֹת.

However, when trying to understand and interpret the Bible, the most important thing is its 'context.' What must be kept in mind here is that this is the Psalm. Thus, it should be considered along with the literary nature of the Psalms that God used the individual intellectual competence and personality of each human writer involved in the writing work of the Bible. In addition, from verse 1 to 5 of Psalm 12 (to verse 6 in the Hebrew Scripture), the psalmist speaks of men's untruthful, proud, and evil words; but in verse 6 (verse 7 in the Hebrew Scripture), he suddenly mentions "the words of the LORD." This is to contrast the untruthful, proud, and evil words of men mentioned above with the "pure words" of God. Therefore, in verse 7 (verse 8 in the Hebrew Scripture), it is clear that "them" the LORD keeps is "the pure words of the LORD": for God will never preserve men's untruthful, proud, and evil words. Therefore, it is the matter of context before that of grammar or syntax, and the grammatical and syntactical interpretation described above must also be understood in this context. All these rationales taken

---

[47] Wilhelm Gesenius, *Gesenius' Hebrew Grammar*, ed. & enl. E. Kautzsch, 2nd English ed. A.E. Cowley from the 28th German ed. (New York: Oxford University Press, 1910), 440.

[48] Young Gil Shin, "God's Promise to Preserve His Word: An Exegetical Study of Psalm 12:5-7" (Master's thesis, Far Eastern Bible College, 1999), 36-37.

[49] Wilhelm Gesenius, *Gesenius' Hebrew Grammar*, 157-158.

together, Psalm 12:6-7 (12:7-8 in the Hebrew Scripture) is definitely the supporting text for the preservation of God's Word.

1.2.2 Literature Review on Verbal Plenary Preservation

Verbal Plenary Preservation, along with Verbal Plenary Inspiration, are the two core doctrines of the Bible. As explained in Verbal Plenary Inspiration, 'verbal' and 'plenary' refer to the 'words' and 'the entirety of the Bible' composed of the 'words,' respectively. Therefore, Verbal Plenary Preservation is God's promise to preserve all His words, which were written by inspiration, purely without any damage. It is also the promise that has lasted from the moment God completed the writings of the Word through the Apostles to the present and forever. The following reviews have been made in connection with this important core doctrine of the Bible - Verbal Plenary Preservation:

George Skariah introduces four prevailing views of the preservation of the Scripture:[50]

First, 'the special providential preservation view': It is a view that many people, from the 16th century reformation, could witness God's providential guidance for the godly men (such as Erasmus, Stephanus, and Beza) to recognize His inspired Word through the Masoretic text for the Old Testament and the *Textus Receptus* for the New (from the Byzantine Text). This view had continued until it was challenged by the modern critics such as Westcott and Hort in the 19th century.

Second, 'the heavenly preservation view': This view is that God preferentially preserves His Word in heaven forever and unchanged. Hence, the proponents of this view claim that God is responsible for preservation of the Word in heaven, and God's people on earth. However, it ignores the original purpose of God's giving of His Word to man (to let the people on earth know God Himself and His will) and the fact that the Subject of preservation is God Himself, not man.

Third, 'essential preservation view': This view, also called the "totality of manuscript," was advocated by some Fundamentalists. It is believed that there is the Word of God somewhere among numerous Greek manuscripts, and this view eventually provided an ammunition for textual criticism. Hence, the proponents of this view think that man is responsible for restoring the preserved Word by finding 'the' manuscript through the application of textual criticism.

Fourth, 'no preservation view': This is the view that completely denies the doctrine of the preservation of the Scripture, and the representative person is Wallace of Dallas Theological Seminary. He accused the doctrine of preservation, of a merely subjective assumption of which is the truth and only a recently created doctrine without a scrutinized exegetical basis. However, this view is based on a humanistic approach to history and faulty biblical hermeneutics.

Skariah conducts a thorough exegetical scriptural analysis on the first view: the special providential preservation view. This is to scripturally substantiate the doctrine of

---

[50] George Skariah, ibid.

preservation, from both the Old and New Testaments. Through the exegetical scriptural analysis, he demonstrates that the preservation of the Scriptures is derived not only for the autographs, but also for the inerrancy and infallibility of the apographs in God's extraordinary providence. Not only that, he shows from his findings that God has perfectly preserved His entire inspired Word (entire preservation) without any dispersion, but through the Hebrew Masoretic Text and the Greek *Textus Receptus* (underlying the King James Version) and through the faithful believers in His Church, who accept all of His Word in faith. Therefore, it is proved once again from his study that the perfect written Word, completed by God's inspiration, is still being delivered into our hands today.

Samuel Eio carries out a historical verification of the constant attacks and plots to do harm to God's written Word.[51] In particular, his study attempts a historical understanding of the preservation of the Bible from the completion of its writing to this day. This is to trace how God's promise of the preservation of His Word has been realized in the real field of history, and to confirm that the God-breathed Word is still valid today. In particular, his study highlights the development of the doctrine of Verbal Plenary Preservation since the 16th century Reformation and the Westminster Confession in the 17th century, and its maintaining process in church history to the 20th century. He establishes the historic presence of the doctrine of Verbal Plenary Preservation within the apographs and the authorized King James Version, and examines how it has been mentioned in systematic theologies to this day. This allows for the discovery of which parts of the doctrine modern perspectives have missed or contaminated, and to see what the doctrinal stance on the doctrine of Verbal Plenary Preservation is today.

According to Eio, in the 16th century, it was a fight against the Roman Catholic Church's challenge to the authority of the Bible based on textual criticism. The issue of the authority and preservation of the Bible, which had no problem from the Apostolic period until the Reformation, was escalated to the fight between the apographs and the Latin Vulgate of the Roman Catholic Church, which insisted on the dual authority. Despite Calvin's affirmation of the self-attestation and self-authentication of the Bible, this fierce fight with the textual critics, including the Roman Catholic Church, on the doctrine of Divine preservation of the Bible continued on through the reaffirmation of the Westminster Confession of Faith in the mid-17th century, and till the early 18th century. However, views of the Bible based on the liberalism and the textual criticism of the 19th-century modern theologians have gradually erased the providential preservation of the Bible from their systematic theologies. Even in some cases, Divine inspiration has also been denied. The issues of the authority and preservation of the Bible are interlinked, but the voices, undoubtedly supporting this important doctrine that God has preserved the whole (plenary) and written words (verbal) of the Bible, are almost gone in theology and denominations today. Instead, rampant are a reliance on human judgment, not the Word

---

[51] Samuel Eio Tze Liang, "Towards a Historical Understanding of the Doctrine of Biblical Preservation" (Master's thesis, Far Eastern Bible College, May 2014).

of God, alongside an abundance of doubt regarding the error and preservation of the Bible and eclecticism to wrap up those doubts.

Studies on Verbal Plenary Preservation are by no means common and really limited to some scholars today. This reflects the situation in which only few advocates of the doctrine of Preservation have been retained since textual criticism took control of academic and religious circles. However, the preservation of the Bible was already affirmed by Jesus Christ Himself. Jeffrey Khoo says that during the earthly ministry of Jesus Christ, the Old Testament words quoted by Jesus Christ many times fully demonstrate the existence of the doctrine of Preservation. At the time of Jesus Christ on earth before the New Testament was completed, the Old Testament was the Bible itself, which had been perfectly preserved by the Israelites (especially by their priests, scribes, and scholars). "One jot or one tittle" mentioned in Matthew 5:18 refers to the smallest letter and a very tiny extension in Hebrew, which Jesus Christ was saying about the certainty of the preservation of His Word through the Old Testament written and transmitted in Hebrew. More than just a simple quotation from the Old Testament, Jesus Christ explained in detail the original meaning of that quoted word (e.g. Matthew 5:21-24). This was possible because the certainty of error-free transmission and preservation of the Old Testament quoted by Him was premised. Thus, Khoo reiterated Edward Hills' words, explaining that it was "an absolutely trustworthy reproduction" of the Old Testament by Jesus Christ. Khoo also proves that the New Testament has been fully preserved by God through His "universal priesthood of believers," who are genuine and faithful Christians as the members of His true Church. This led to the *Textus Receptus* with the development of printing technology, which is the Word of the New Testament that has been preserved by God with His special providential care, underlying today's King James Version. In God's providence, the process of preservation leading to the *Textus Receptus* is a collaboration of the faith, circumstances, and also manuscripts that God has preserved.[52] In this same context, Dean Burgon said that in God's providence, the preservation of His written Word (especially focusing on the New Testament Gospels) has been made in peculiarly varied ways to preserve its integrity: First, God, in the safest way from fraud, has kept His Word through multiple copies. These copies are the majority texts[53] that have been used in His Church, representing the sacred autographs

---

[52] Jeffrey Khoo, *Kept Pure in All Ages*, 33-36.

[53] Alan J. Hauser and Duane F. Watson, ed., *A History of Biblical Interpretation, Volume 2: The Medieval through the Reformation Periods* (Grand Rapids, Michigan: William B. Eerdmans Publishing Company, 2009), 229-230. Unlike the critical texts, the majority Greek texts, called the Byzantine texts, had been used in the Eastern churches centring on Constantinople. Then, those majority texts, which had been preserved and used in the Eastern churches, were introduced into the Western churches through various paths such as the Crusades. Only then, the majority texts were recognized again by the Western churches, around the fall of Constantinople (1453) in the mid-15th century. This was possible because the Greek-speaking personnel, along with the majority texts, were also brought into the Western churches. Thus, the apographs that had been carrying on the legacy of the autographs did not 'disappear and suddenly appear again one day'; it had not yet been discovered by the Western churches during the disconnection period between the Western and Eastern churches. This is a fact that history proves. Rather, the corrupted manuscripts, which textual criticism claims to be the older, were of no use by the churches at that time.

themselves, self-evident and without any doubt; Second, there have been the Bible versions based on the need to be translated into various languages for use in different branches of the early churches. There are many authentic records of the existence of the New Testament during the first centuries of the Christian era; Third, the fact that the early church fathers quoted the existing codices (which they were personally familiar with) many times at that time is also a testimony to the contents of and a safeguard of its integrity of the Bible that God wrote and left in the hands of men.[54]

Paul Ferguson discusses the historical positions on Verbal Plenary Preservation from the Reformers to the present day. In the providence of God, the Beginner and Controller of human history, the Reformation was the opportunity to enthrone the Bible again out of the dark ages. This was facilitated by the widespread use of the received text with the development of printing technology, and under the consensus of the reformers to the core doctrines of the 66 books. The issue of Bible preservation also adhered to the received text, based on the reformers' unwavering confession of faith that God's inspired Word, from the autographs to the apographs, has been preserved by God Himself, the very original Author, not others. Their confession of faith was thoroughly observed through '*Sola Scriptura*.' Of course, the Preserver and Guardian of God's Word is its original Author, God Himself; but the reformers including Calvin, who belonged to His Church universal, had fought their hearts out as the faithful and sincere witnesses to the Word. Nevertheless, the textual critics condemned their efforts for the Bible as "bibliolatry," and the received text was attacked by the Roman Catholic Church, for the Catholic Church recognized only Jerome's Latin Vulgate as the authentic Bible. Then, came the Revised Version and textual criticism under the advocacy of the Roman Catholic Church, which is based on human reason and science, not in God. Nevertheless, during the Reformation and post-Reformation periods, all Bible translations by the reformers were thoroughly of the received text, not of the critics with doubts on the apographs. Their true beliefs related to the preservation of the Word are also very well expressed in the Westminster Confession of Faith (1643-1648) and the *Formula Consensus Helvetica* (1675).

However, these reformative efforts based on the absolute belief in God's absolute Word, the Bible, escalated into sharper confrontations with the modernists and the liberals in the 19th and 20th centuries after the introduction of Modernism in the 18th century. The liberals such as Briggs and Hort even fiercely attacked Divine inspiration and inerrancy of the written Word, even not hesitating to utter blasphemous remarks, saying "human search precedes Divine revelation." The modernists and the liberals emphasize that a rationalistic and skeptical approach to the Bible must be taken. Only then can it be said to be 'acceptable' as God's inspired Word. This is just a subtle whispering, looking at the Bible from a perspective thoroughly based on textual criticism,

---

Thus, they were found by a close call, just before being discarded by the churches because of their valuelessness in use. The critics are now claiming it as authentic just because it is older.

[54] John W. Burgon, *The Revision Revised: A Refutation of Westcott and Hort's False Greek Text and Theory* (Collingswood, New Jersey: Dean Burgon Society Press, 1883), 8-9.

to turn their eyes from the apparently extant perfect Bible by the perfect preservation of God, its original Author, and eventually to make them deny it on the pretext of finding the originals. While the modernists and the liberals have been trying to fit Divine inspiration into their modern view based on higher criticism in the name of demythologization, it is, after all, a pun and reckless attempt to disregard and confine the intentions and providences of the Triune God, the original Author of the Bible, under the limits of human reason. In the world occupied by the modernists and the liberals, the perfect preserved Bible of God is no longer God's 'absolute' Word to them, and it is just to deal with the Bible as no different from other human literatures, by saying that the Word of God 'becomes' in accordance with human standards.

Thus, the doctrine of the perfect inspiration and preservation of the Word of God was the universal view of the Christian world, until textual criticism, boasting its short history, shook theology with the influence of rationalism emerging alongside 18th-century Modernism. In particular, the modernists and the liberals have raised a strong question about the fact that the autographs which God wrote by His inspiration have been preserved equally inerrant and infallible through the faithful apographs. The lack of faith in God's promise of the providential preservation of the Word is the driving force that has made the critics continue their fruitless works of textual criticism. For them, evidence-based academic search is more important than doctrinal certainty based on God's Word. They thoroughly reject the presuppositional beliefs and thoughts based on the Bible. These absolute doctrines of the perfect inspiration and preservation about the Bible, especially the preservation matter, are ignored today even by the new fundamentalists and set aside as the targets for total suspicion. Even with advocacy and toleration of the critical texts, the historic view of perfect preservation has been the target of their heavy blows. Turning their backs against the preservation of the Word is the same as saying openly that God's certain promise to preserve His Word has completely failed. This is to mock the infinite Word of God, leaning on limited human reason and scholarship. Their unbelief in God's absolute Word and their methodological premises of textual criticism eventually led them to the tragic conclusion that they do not know where God's Word is. Their attitude is the same for the King James Version, the most accurate and faithful translation based on God's preserved apographs (the Hebrew Masoretic Text for the Old Testament; the Greek *Textus Receptus* for the New Testament). The modernists and the liberals, i.e. the textual critics, lack the certainty of God's Word: as they themselves claim, 'for them' there is no certain Word in existence that God Himself wrote and has preserved.[55]

---

[55] P. S. Ferguson, "The Historic Views of the Church Concerning Preservation," *Confessional Bibliology Blog*, retrieved May 19, 2020, https://confessionalbibliology.com/wp-content/uploads/2016/04/pb-preservation-quotes.pdf.

<u>Counterarguments on Preservation and Problem:</u>
<u>Textual Criticism and Verbal Plenary Preservation</u>

The Enlightenment, which emerged in Europe in the 17th and 18th centuries, denied anything transcendental beyond human reason and attempted to understand everything within the limits of reason. In keeping with that, the Christian faith as well as the Bible, which had been regarded as an absolute value until that time, were also considered as the objects of reinterpretation and re-evaluation based on human reason. In the meantime, the modern biblical criticism was also beginning to come up. After the first printed Greek text of Erasmus in the16th century, the proposition that had been considered in the Church without any need for discussion was that the *Textus Receptus* was the very Word of God, with the obvious fact that it was written by God's inspiration through the penning of the Apostles, inerrant and infallible, and had been preserved by God and transmitted through His faithful Church. Here, the theological approach was applied on the premise that, following Erasmus, the *Textus Receptus* was edited in accordance to the divine providence and guidance of God. However, all these things were denied with the rise of the skepticism based on the naturalistic textual criticism following 17th-century rationalism and 18th-century enlightenment. The assumptions of those 'isms' were completely dependent on human thought and rationality. For example, Bengel formulated the rule of "the harder reading is to be preferred to the easy reading." And Griesbach, based on Bengel's formula, additionally formulated the rule that, of the many variant readings in one place, the reading which preferred the orthodox dogma was questionable. His skepticism that all extant New Testament texts were just the editorial revisions of the critical texts, which were damaged by Christians, had deeply influenced later the ideas of many codicologists. Also, Semler, who claimed himself as the "one of the first modernists," argued for artificial editing by the ancient scribes, denying Divine inspiration itself. This modernistic skepticism culminated in the mid-19th century, with two manuscripts (*Aleph* א and *B*) that were made available by Tregelles and Tischendorf's efforts, introduced by Westcott and Hort as the almost complete reproduction of the original New Testament. The corruption theory of the early days and skepticism were again popular among the modernists, as Westcott and Hort actually followed Griesbach's opinion along with a refutation to the accessibility to the original texts; and they have continued to this day. Nevertheless, the corrupted manuscripts introduced by Westcott and Hort have continued to be the foundations and subjects of major theological studies. All such theories that deny and criticize this traditional theological approach basically exclude the two doctrines of the Bible themselves – Divine inspiration and providential preservation of the Bible. All of these serious symptoms originated from the attempt to tamper with the Word with human thoughts, judgments, and standards, instead of believing God's promise that He Himself has preserved His Word written by Himself. In all these doubts and arbitrary assumptions, there is a heavily layered distrust in God's providential preservation and a groundless assertion of the critical texts by men. However, it is very ironic that their skepticism is rather becoming an attempt to mutilate the true texts that God has preserved.[56]

Textual criticism is one of the philosophical arts that was originally applied to the general science, and its history dates back to the preservation matter of the ancient works by the librarians of Hellenistic Alexandria in the 2nd century BC. Then, going through the Middle Ages with the invention of the printing press, it had gotten to the early modern age. Textual criticism is part of an academic activity to screen the 'text' of an original by comparing its copies, when there are multiple copies of an original.[57] In other words, it is an attempt to reconstruct and maintain the 'text' to be closest to the original one by comparing and analyzing differences included in the texts of several copies.[58] In fact, all these efforts are due to the problem that the originals no longer exist. Thus, textual criticism can be defined as the science and art to determine "the most reliable wording of a text" by comparing its manuscripts.[59]

The two main methodologies of textual criticism, which had been practiced by the editors of the ancient Greek, are 'recension' and 'emendation': the former is to select the most reliable evidence to be the basis of the text, after reviewing all possible sources. The latter means an attempt to eliminate errors found even in the best manuscripts.[60] The application of the important methods to the editing of the classical texts was developed by three German scholars - Imrichi Bekker (1785-1871, one of the founders of classical philosophy), Karl Lachmann (1793-1851), and Friedrich Wolf (1759-1824). Since then, several scholars had gone through various discussions on the important rules to keep in mind when implementing textual criticism upon this basic methodology:[61] First, the principles of textual criticism, which are most fundamentally mentioned, are as follows. These principles are summarized by Finegan in his book, as 'the Canons of Tischendorf (1815-1874)' which describe a total of six principles:[62]

> (1) the text is to be sought from the most ancient evidence, meaning especially the oldest Greek manuscripts; (2) a reading peculiar to a single document is to be considered suspect; (3) an obvious scribal error is to be rejected even though well supported in the manuscripts; (4) in parallel passages the tendency of copyists would be to make the readings agree, and therefore, in such passages, testimonies are to be preferred which are not in precise accordance; (5) that reading is to be preferred which could have given occasion to the others, or which appears to

---

[56] Edward F. Hills, *The King James Version Defended* (Des Moines, Iowa: The Christian Research Press, 1984), 62-67.

[57] S. Michael Houdmann, ed., *Questions about the Bible: The 100 Most Frequently Asked Questions about the Bible* (Edinburgh, Scotland: WestBow Press, 2015), 147.

[58] Stanley E. Porter and Andrew W. Pitts, *Fundamentals of New Testament Textual Criticism* (Grand Rapids, Michigan: William B. Eerdmans Publishing Company, 2015), 1-3.

[59] Paul D. Wegner, *A Student's Guide to Textual Criticism of the Bible: Its History, Methods and Results* (Downers Grove, Illinois: InterVarsity Press, 2006), 24.

[60] Bruce M. Metzger and Bart D. Ehrman, *The Text of New Testament* (New York, Oxford: Oxford University Press, 2005), 205.

[61] "Rules of Textual Criticism," Bible Research, accessed on March 18, 2020, http://www.bible-researcher.com/rules.html.

[62] Jack Finegan, *Encountering New Testament Manuscripts: A Working Introduction to Textual Criticism* (Grand Rapids, Michigan: William B. Eerdmans Publishing Company, 1980), 63.

comprise the elements of the others; and (6) that reading is to be preferred which accords with NT Greek or with the style of the individual writer.

Next, Metzger and Ehrman claimed Eclecticism, stating that both external and internal evidences were required as the criteria for the judgment when performing textual criticism.[63] This is part of Evidentialism based on Modernism. In addition, Kurt Aland and Barbara Aland had presented twelve basic rules for the New Testament textual criticism.[64] The rules of Aland and Aland are basically based on doubts about and unbelief in the fact that God has preserved the originals (autographs), which was written by His inspiration, through the copies (apographs) in the same inerrant and infallible way. Because they deny the existence of the perfectly preserved apographs by God Himself through His faithful Church, they basically presuppose the variant readings of the original texts in the process of textual criticism; and thus, Evidentialism is inevitably intervened to determine whether or not those readings can be the originals. And they predict the possibility of the original texts by their arbitrary standards based on human reason and experiences: a representative standard is 'the preference for the harder and shorter reading.' However, this is only their assumption, and the idea of restoring the original truths on the assumption does not make sense.

Such logics of the critics stand against the principle of Divine preservation, what God promised. In the 18th century, as challenged by rational textual criticism, the debates about the doctrine of Preservation began to emerge. Until then, Verbal Plenary Inspiration and Preservation of God's written Word were the historical doctrines that the Church held to.[65] However, the issue of Verbal Plenary Preservation, triggered by the influence of Modernism that relies on human reason, has continued to be a target of the debates to this day. This is because even theologians who acknowledge Verbal Plenary Inspiration have doubts that God has preserved His written Word until now. Some of them even deny that the Word of God is still perfectly preserved today, and look at the Bible we have today, presuming that it is impossible at all. Then, to evaluate the Bible, they use textual criticism. Therefore, it is textual criticism that must be addressed with regard to Verbal Plenary Preservation.

Depending on Human Reasoning

The biggest problem with textual criticism lies in its criteria for the judgment: it relies strictly on human reasoning and not on the absolute truth of God. Nevertheless, judging God's Word based on human reason is nothing more than putting human reason above God's Word.[66] But human reason is not absolute: it is relative and varies depending on the environments and circumstances, which means that the Word of God is often

---

[63] Metzger and Ehrman, *The Text of New Testament*, 301-304.

[64] Kurt Aland and Barbara Aland, *The Text of the New Testament: As Introduction to the Critical Editions and to the Theory and Practice of Textual Criticism*, 2nd ed., trans. Erroll F. Rhodes (Grand Rapids, Michigan: William B. Eerdmans Publishing Co., 1989), 280-281.

[65] Ferguson, 5.

[66] Henk van den Belt, *The Authority of Scripture in Reformed Theology: Truth and Trust* (Leiden, Boston: Brill, 2008), 329.

evaluated in different ways from an extremely subjective point of view according to human reason. Therefore, human reason cannot be a standard for judging the Word of God. Since the Bible is the Word of God written by the inspiration of the Holy Spirit (2 Tim 3:16), its contents themselves are already absolute, following the immutability of God, its original Author (Mal 3:6, "For I am the LORD, I change not"). The Word of God is truth (Jn 17:17, "thy word is truth"), never changes (1 Sam 15:29, "the Strength of Israel will not lie nor repent: for he is not a man, that he should repent"), and absolute. Psalm 111:7-8 says: "The works of his hands are verity and judgment; all his commandments are sure. They stand fast for ever and ever, and are done in truth and uprightness." Thus, the Westminster Confession of Faith Chapter 1.4 says that the Word of God, the only truth, not human reason, is the only criterion of the judgment for all: "The authority of the holy scripture, for which it ought to be believed, and obeyed, dependeth not upon the testimony of any man, or church; but wholly upon God, (who is truth itself,) the author thereof; and therefore it is to be received, because it is the Word of God."[67]

Unbelief in God's Promises on Divine Preservation

Also, another problem with textual criticism is that the critics do not believe God's promise to preserve His Word perfectly. God has already promised in the Bible about the preservation of His Word:

> *"For verily I say unto you, Till heaven and earth pass, one jot or one tittle shall in no wise pass from the law, till all be fulfilled"* (Mt 5:18)
> *"Heaven and earth shall pass away, but my words shall not pass away"* (Mt 24:35)
> *"The words of the LORD are pure words: as silver tried in a furnace of earth, purified seven times. Thou shalt keep them, O LORD, thou shalt preserve them from this generation for ever"* (Ps 12:6-7)
> *"Being born again, not of corruptible seed, but of incorruptible, by the word of God, which liveth and abideth for ever. For all flesh is as grass, and all the glory of man as the flower of grass. The grass withereth, and the flower thereof falleth away: But the word of the Lord endureth for ever. And this is the word which by the gospel is preached unto you"* (1 Pet 1:23-25)

Therefore, it is ultimately the unbelief in God's promise that textual criticism criticizes and arbitrarily fabricates the Bible under the pretext of a reading close to the original texts. God sternly warned that His Word must not be interpreted indiscreetly or arbitrarily by man.: "Knowing this first, that no prophecy of the scripture is of any private interpretation. For the prophecy came not in old time by the will of man: but holy men of God spake as they were moved by the Holy Ghost" (2 Pet 1:20-21). In addition to the stern warning against man's arbitrary alteration of His Word, God also forewarned against every attempt to alter His Word: "For I testify unto every man that heareth the words of the prophecy of this book, If any man shall add unto these things, God shall add unto him the plagues that are written in this book: And if any man shall take away from

---

[67] "Westminster Confession of Faith Chapter 1: Of the Holy Scripture - no.4," Bible Presbyterian Church General Synod, accessed on March 22, 2020, https://bpc.org/?page_id=542.

the words of the book of this prophecy, God shall take away his part out of the book of life, and out of the holy city, and from the things which are written in this book" (Rev 22:18-19). Therefore, based on God's Word, textual criticism itself, which arbitrarily judges and interprets the Bible according to human reason and even recklessly alters it, is already against the Word and is the unbelief in God's promise of Preservation.

Unbelief in Divine Preservation Is the Unbelief in Divine Inspiration

The unbelief in Divine preservation eventually leads to the unbelief in Divine inspiration. Some textual critics claim to hold to Divine inspiration, but their denial of God's preservation of His inspired Word to this day yields the conclusion that it is impossible to know which one was written by Divine inspiration. Therefore, it boils down to the unbelief in and denial of Divine inspiration as well as Divine preservation. For example, Metzger and Ehrman's eclectic view addresses the problem of the Synoptic Gospels. In other words, to say that the Gospel of Mark is the source of two other Gospels (Matthew and Luke) is already carrying out textual criticism with doubts about Inspiration as well as Preservation. The problem of the Synoptic Gospels is not the problem of which book is the first and the source. It does not acknowledge the fact that God moved the four writers of the four Gospels to record the four aspects of Jesus Christ. That is, the textual critics do not accept that the original Author of the four Gospels is God Himself, and within the limits of human thinking, they arbitrarily assume that there must be a human writer who served as the source. This is a denial that God inspired, wrote one by one, and has preserved the four Gospels without any change to this day; This is the thought and act that undermine the Word of God, the perfect Bible, and that blaspheme God's all-knowing (omniscience) and all-powerful (omnipotence). Divine preservation is based upon Divine inspiration. Divine inspiration is not valid without Divine preservation:[68] these two must go together. However, textual criticism is a double negation of these two core doctrines of the Bible, which are directly witnessed by God Himself as its original Author.

<u>Further Discussion: Textual Criticism, Unbelief in Verbal Plenary Preservation, and the Denial of the Activating Ground of the Holy Spirit's Illumination</u>

Another issue that must be considered in relation to the logic of the modern critics is the illumination of the Holy Spirit. Before the ascension of Jesus Christ, He repeatedly said that He would send "another Comforter," the Holy Spirit. John 14:16 says: "And I will pray the Father, and he shall give you another Comforter, that he may abide with you for ever." Also, verse 26 of the same chapter clearly shows the functional hierarchy within the Triune God, where God the Father sends God the Holy Spirit in the name of God the Son. Also, in John 15:26, Jesus Christ says that He is the One who sends the Holy Spirit. In addition, Jesus Christ describes what the Holy Spirit does, that is, the

---

[68] Jeffrey Khoo, *Kept Pure in All Ages*, 15.

role of the Holy Spirit. Thus, the following statements of Jesus Christ in this regard need to be remembered:

> *"But the Comforter, which is the Holy Ghost, whom the Father will send in my name, he shall teach you all things, and bring all things to your remembrance, whatsoever I have said unto you"* (Jn 14:26)
>
> *"But when the Comforter is come, whom I will send unto you from the Father, even the Spirit of truth, which proceedeth from the Father, he shall testify of me"* (Jn 15:26)

First, the characteristic of the Holy Spirit revealed in John 15:26 is "the Spirit of truth." Here, the Greek word τῆς ἀληθείας corresponding to "of truth" can be seen as "the ablative of purpose" in its case. In terms of Verbal Plenary Inspiration, it is the Holy Spirit that inspired all the words (even the smallest points) of the Scriptures, by guiding the human writers to pen without any error or mistake (2 Pet 1:21; 2 Tim 3:16). In particular, Jesus Christ said of the Holy Spirit that He would be sent in the name of Jesus Christ ("in my name") to testify of Jesus Christ ("shall testify of me"). In addition, Jesus Christ also said in John 14:26 that the Holy Spirit would teach and make remember all that He had said. Here, it is necessary to consider who received this promise - that is, the referent of "you." This "you" used for these verses in the Greek Scriptures are all second person plural pronouns. And considering the context, when Jesus Christ said this, it was the place where He gave the last supper to His disciples just before He was caught in the evening of Passover. There, the listeners (in plural) were none other than the disciples of Jesus Christ. Therefore, it would be more reasonable to regard this promise of the Holy Spirit as the promise predicated on the special mission of the disciples of Jesus Christ, rather than as given in a general sense. Another point to think about is the expression, used when giving this promise to His disciples, that Jesus Christ "will send" the Holy Spirit. Peter and the other disciples of Jesus Christ, with the exception of Judas Iscariot, were already those who confessed Jesus Christ as their Savior (Jn 6:68-71).[69] Therefore, the Holy Spirit was already indwelling in them. Nevertheless, this saying of Jesus Christ ("will send" again the Holy Spirit to His disciples) suggests that it is related to the aspects other than their faith. In particular, it should be noted that the preposition used in the Greek Scriptures in connection with the advent of the Holy Spirit is ἐπι, not εἰς. This is the same preposition that is used at the baptism of Jesus Christ (Mt 3:16; Mk 1:10; Lk 3:22; Jn 1:32) as well as at the coming down of the Holy Spirit He promised His disciples (Acts 2:3; 10:44; 19:6). The King James translators applied the same "upon" to ἐπι in the corresponding verses, indicating that the Holy Spirit stayed "upon" the person in a 'functional' sense rather than in the sense of being indwelling the saved following their salvation.[70]

---

[69] "Then Simon Peter answered him, <u>Lord</u>, to whom shall we go? <u>thou hast the words of eternal life. And we believe and are sure that thou art that Christ, the Son of the living God.</u> Jesus answered them, Have not I chosen you twelve, and one of you is a devil? He spake of Judas Iscariot the son of Simon: for he it was that should betray him, being one of the twelve" (Jn 6:68-71; <u>emphasis added</u>)

[70] If εἰς is applied to these verses, this leads to serious heretical thoughts; For example, if εἰς is applied to the coming down of the Holy Spirit at the baptism of Jesus Christ, it first violates the doctrine of

This phraseology was also used by Jesus Christ Himself, who promised the coming down of the Holy Spirit in Acts 1:8 (ἐπελθόντος τοῦ Ἁγίου Πνεύματος ἐφ᾽ ὑμᾶς). Here, three verbal phrases in this verse ("the Holy Ghost is come upon" - "receive power" - "be witnesses unto me") show the functional connection of the coming down of the Holy Spirit and its subsequent procedures. The coming down of the Holy Spirit in a functional sense is also observed in the Old Testament. Its representative examples are Saul and David as the kings of Israel. Just after Saul was anointed as a king in 1 Samuel 10:1, he received the Holy Spirit in verse 6 ("the Spirit of the LORD will come upon thee"). The Hebrew preposition used here for "upon" is עַל, indicating the stay of the Holy Spirit upon Saul, who became the first king of Israel. On the other hand, in 1 Samuel 16:13, the same expression is used as soon as David was anointed as the second king of Israel ("the Spirit of the LORD came upon David"). In contrast, it is also recorded in the immediately following verse 14 that the Holy Spirit had left Saul ("the Spirit of the LORD departed from Saul"). At this time, unlike 1 Samuel 10:6, the preposition אֶל (upon; unto, toward) is used here in 1 Samuel 16:13, although it is translated as the same "upon." This can be said to emphasize the 'direction' of the functional coming down of the Holy Spirit, following the shift of the kingly office from Saul to David, with the preposition מֵעִם (from) of verse 14. As such, the coming down of the Holy Spirit in the above verses is for carrying out the offices and functions God had entrusted to His servants, apart from the salvation matter of each individual.

Jeffrey Khoo says that Jesus Christ's disciples were "filled with the Holy Ghost" on the day of Pentecost as the fulfillment of His promise (Acts 2:4) – it has to do not with their salvation, but with their "service": that is, their special mission they must fulfill after the ascension of Jesus Christ. It was their ministry for the words of Jesus Christ.[71] The culminating part of His disciples' Word ministry is to complete the entire 66 books through the writing of the Bible, that is, the completion of the New Testament. What must be their ministry is also well revealed in the words of Jesus Christ in John 16:13-15.[72] In verses 14 and 15, Jesus Christ says that the Holy Spirit "shall receive/take of mine" and let the disciples know about it. In particular, in verse 13, the saying that the Holy Spirit would show "things to come" to the disciples means that the disciples' mission would be

---

the Holy Trinity: three distinctive persons in one God. In addition, it is also a serious heretical idea that applies the principles of man, who is a creature of God as well as the object of salvation, to Jesus Christ, who is the perfect God as well as the perfect Man and also the Saviour (However, unlike the *Textus Receptus*, the Nestle-Aland Greek text applies εἰς instead of ἐπι for Mark 1:10). Moreover, since the disciples of Jesus Christ, except for Judas Iscariot, were already those who had faith and confession of it, the Holy Spirit was already indwelling in them. Therefore, ἐπι used in the Book of Acts should also be regarded as a 'functional' coming down of the Holy Spirit upon the disciples of Jesus Christ related to their 'Word' ministry. The cases of Cornelius and John the Baptist's disciples should also be understood in the same context.

[71] Jeffrey Khoo, *Charismatism Q&A: Biblical Answers to Frequently Asked Questions on the Charismatic Phenomenon* (Singapore: Far Eastern Bible College Press, 1999), 21-22.

[72] "Howbeit when he, the Spirit of truth, is come, he will guide you into all truth: for he shall not speak of himself; but whatsoever he shall hear, that shall he speak: and he will shew you things to come. He shall glorify me: for he shall receive of mine, and shall shew it unto you. All things that the Father hath are mine: therefore said I, that he shall take of mine, and shall shew it unto you" (Jn 16:13-15)

beyond the preaching and teaching according to "the Great Commission" of Jesus Christ (Mt 28:18-20). That is, their mission would also include writing in the Bible about future things to come after the fulfillment of Jesus Christ's earthly ministry. And in the penning of the Scriptures by the disciples, it was manifested as the inspiration of the Holy Spirit to the Word of God. As can be seen in the scene of Moses receiving the Word directly from God, God's presence and intervention in the writing of God's Word is observed in many places in the Old Testament as well as in the New Testament. Therefore, the coming down of the Holy Spirit promised to the disciples is a functional coming down related to the writing and completion of the Word of truth, and the Holy Spirit has an inseparable relationship with Jesus Christ, who is the truth. Moreover, the Verbal Plenary Inspiration and Preservation of the Scriptures are the core doctrines of the Bible that must be applied to the entire Bible from the Old Testament to the New Testament. In the writing of the Bible by the human writers, the moving and guiding of the Holy Spirit had been consistently applied from Moses, the author of the first Scriptures of the Old Testament, to the Apostle John, the author of the last Scripture of the New Testament. Also, the expression of 'the written Scriptures' is not applied only after the completion of the entire 66 books, but has been continuously applied in the process of God's progressive revelation and its final product to this present day: of course, the Subject of inspiration and preservation, all is God. The 66 books of the Holy Scriptures are the complete collection of truths, and the original Author and Subject of their preservation is none other than God Himself. When considering this fact, it should not be forgotten that the activities of the Holy Spirit, which Jesus Christ promised through His disciples, also takes place on the firm foundation of the 66 books of the Holy Scriptures. What Jesus Christ said in John 14:26 and 15:26 also shows that the illumination of the Holy Spirit is manifested on the foundation of the perfect Bible, which God wrote through His prophets and apostles, the human writers, and has preserved through His faithful Church. This is also the testimony of the Apostle Paul in Ephesians 2:20-22: "And are built upon the foundation of the apostles and prophets, Jesus Christ himself being the chief corner stone; In whom all the building fitly framed together groweth unto an holy temple in the Lord: In whom ye also are builded together for an habitation of God through the Spirit." Here, "the foundation of the apostles and prophets" denotes the entire Old and New Testaments, and the Church of Jesus Christ is built on the foundation of these entire Testaments "through the Spirit." This function of the Holy Spirit, His illumination of God's Word, remains the same today. Therefore, the denial of Verbal Plenary Inspiration and Preservation, which God directs, is also the denial of the illumination of the Holy Spirit. The Holy Spirit is "the Spirit of truth" that works only on the truth of God (Jn 16:13). Nevertheless, the modern critics' claim that the perfect Bible does not exist anymore today is to deny the truth itself, the foundation of the Spirit's activities as Jesus Christ said. And their claim denying the fact that God has perfectly preserved His written Word to this day without error is the same as denying the possibility of the Spirit's activities themselves. It is because God's truth cannot be in error, and "the Spirit of truth," the Holy Spirit, cannot take His actions on error other than 'the' truth of God: being inspired and having perfectly preserved by God

Himself. Therefore, this unbelieving view and attitude of the modern critics is very blasphemous, denying the following: God's omniscience and omnipotence, and also His providential care of His Word; the promise of Jesus Christ who is the truth itself and the living Word; and the illumination of the Holy Spirit who is sent by God the Father and God the Son; in particular, when focusing on the fact that the promise of the Holy Spirit that Jesus Christ gave to His disciples is, above all else, an emphasis on the functional role of the Holy Spirit for the entire written Word and its completion.

1.3 Verbal Plenary Inspiration, Verbal Plenary Preservation, and Textual Criticism

The two core doctrines of the Bible, Verbal Plenary Inspiration and Verbal Plenary Preservation, are interlinked and inseparable. God had progressively revealed His will through the prophets and the apostles. This had been consistent since the creation of the world and the fall of the first man by the sin of disobedience, beginning with the very first gospel God Himself proclaimed. From God's eternal decree, His revelation from the beginning to the end is of Jesus Christ, who is the Savior of man as God Himself as well as the perfect Man. And the revelation ends with the words of the Book of Revelation about the second coming, judgment, and eternal reign of Jesus Christ. Hence, God Himself wrote His written Word as the perfect completion of His progressive and constant revelations. That is the Bible, the 66 books from Genesis to Revelation. Although the prophets and apostles were used as the instruments for penning the Bible, its original Author is definitely God Himself, the Subject of all those revelations (Verbal Plenary Inspiration, 2 Tim 3:16); And there has been no further revelation since the completion of the Bible (Rev 22:18-19), because it is enough: necessary and sufficient for all.

Also, for the Bible God Himself wrote, God also promised its perfect preservation (Ps 12:6-7; Mt 5:18). This is, in a way, a necessary promise. It is because, if God's written Word is not perfectly preserved as in the first place, there is no guarantee of the original Word He Himself inspired. It is God's will that the same message be passed from generation to generation as it was first written, so that all men of all ages can reach the very same truth of Jesus Christ, the blessed message of salvation through Him, and the warning of His judgment (Jn 3:16-21; God's desiderative will[73]). Such intention of God, the original Author of the Bible, is well reflected in the Great Commission, which was last given to the apostles and disciples of Jesus Christ just before He ascended (Mt 28:18-20; Acts 1:8). Also, God's Word is completely interconnected without any error or contradiction. The perfection of God's Word that transcends the limits of human reason and intellect is evident through the warning of the Apostle Peter: "Knowing this first, that no prophecy of the scripture is of any private interpretation. For the prophecy came not in old time by the will of man: but holy men of God spake as they were moved by the Holy Ghost." (2 Pet 1:20-21). In verse 20, the Greek word used for "any private" is ἰδίας, which means "one's own." That is, it is forbidden for man to interpret the Word indiscreetly and arbitrarily on his own terms. The reason is well explained in the immediately following verse 21, "spake as they

---

[73] Timothy Tow, *The Clock of the Sevenfold Will of God* (Singapore: Far Eastern Bible College Press, 1991), 40-46.

were moved by the Holy Spirit." In other words, the prohibition of arbitrary self-interpretation by man paradoxically shows that the whole of the Word of God is completely and organically connected in itself, based on the fact that the principle of writing the Bible is Verbal Plenary Inspiration. Therefore, it is impossible for any imperfect and fallible man to arbitrarily take measure for the preservation process of the perfect Word of God, which cannot be arbitrarily judged or carelessly handled by man. In particular, it was only through God's total superintendence that no damage was made to the inerrancy and infallibility of the Bible during the transmission periods of the Bible through the transcription process until the printing press was invented. Ironically, that is why the critics do not believe in and attack the inerrancy and infallibility of the Bible today. Because the critics' views are thoroughly focused on human reason and practice, they argue that the perfect and complete preservation of the Bible is impossible. The critics do not bear in mind that the Subject of preservation is God Himself. However, this is the very point where the knowledge of and faith in God's omnipotence and His promise are required. God has perfectly preserved His written Word so far without any damage by His singular providential care. Just as God used the human writers as His penmen to write His words, so He has also used His faithful and true Church as the instrument in the preservation process of His words; and the very same words as the originals (autographs) have been preserved to this day through their exactly identical copies (apographs: the Masoretic Text for the Old Testament Hebrew Scriptures and the *Textus Receptus* for the New Testament Greek Scriptures). Therefore, the perfect Bible transmitted to our hands through the perfect preservation by God is exactly the same as that written by God's inspiration through His prophets and apostles.

As such, Verbal Plenary Preservation presupposes Verbal Plenary Inspiration. It is not the Word of God that its inspiration is not premised, because God has already declared that He wrote His Word by His inspiration (2 Tim 3:16; 2 Pet 1:21). Therefore, Verbal Plenary Preservation without Verbal Plenary Inspiration is meaningless. On the other hand, Verbal Plenary Inspiration is valid only when Verbal Plenary Preservation is guaranteed. If God had not preserved the Word He inspired, in other words, if His Word, which was written and completed by the Holy Spirit's inspiration, was no longer preserved after its completion, the extant Bible today would not be the Word God inspired. Since Divine inspiration guarantees the Bible as 'God's Word,' of which the original Author is God Himself, the authenticity of the Bible as 'God's Word' cannot be guaranteed without Divine preservation. Therefore, "perfect inspiration without perfect preservation would leave inspiration a worthless Biblical doctrine."[74] In this way, Verbal Plenary Inspiration and Verbal Plenary Preservation are inextricably linked to each other. Taking this one step further, the illumination of the Holy Spirit takes place only on the basis of the Word, God's truth, which He inspired and has preserved. In other words, the premise of the illumination of the Holy Spirit is also Verbal Plenary Inspiration and Preservation.

---

[74] Kent Brandenburg, ed., *Thou Shalt Keep Them* (El Sobrante, California: Pillar & Ground Publishing, 2003), 68.

CHAPTER II. GOD'S PROMISE AND HUMAN RESPONSIBILITY: VERBAL PLENARY PRESERVATION AND THE LAW OF INALTERABILITY

2.1 Biblical Definition and Features of Truth

2.1.1 Definition of Truth

The general dictionary definition of 'truth' is "the quality of being true"[75] or "a judgment, proposition, or idea that is true or accepted as true." Here, 'TRUTH' written in capital letters is used to mean "a transcendent fundamental or spiritual reality" or "God" Himself.[76] However, the 'truth' that this study is trying to examine is not in the general sense of being recognized and accepted by people, but in the 'absolute' sense that God reveals through His Word. Therefore, according to the teachings of the Bible, MacArthur defines 'truth' as follows: "truth is that which is consistent with the mind, will, character, glory, and being of God." He further goes on to say that 'truth' is "the self-expression of God," adding that it is therefore theological and ontological as well in the sense that it expresses everything as it is. This is possible because 'truth' is entirely the reality and reflection of God. So, God is "the author, source, determiner, governor, arbiter, ultimate standard, and final judge of all truth."[77] It is clearly understood with the fact that, as the Bible describes God as the "God of truth" (Deut 32:4; Ps 31:5; Isa 65:16), the second and third persons of the Triune God are all stated as 'truth.'

The First Person of the Holy Trinity: Truth as the Source of Truth

As already reviewed above, the Bible repeatedly declares the obviousness of the fact that the Triune God is the "God of truth." It is also evident that 'truth' is included in God's attributes which are defined in Westminster Shorter Catechism Question No.4.[78] However, at the same time, in the functional hierarchy of the Triune God, the Bible continues to provide a hint that God the Father is the Source of that 'truth.' First, Jesus Christ says in John 17:17, "thy word is truth." Here, "thy word" representing the Word of God is none other than Jesus Christ Himself. However, in the verse 18 immediately following, Jesus Christ says that it is God the Father who sent Him, God the Son as God's living Word, to the world. In other words, Jesus Christ (God's Word itself) is the truth, which means that He was sent from God the Father who is also the truth. Since truth produces truth, it eventually indicates that God the Father is truth. This is also observed

---

75 "Truth," Cambridge Dictionary, accessed on May 10, 2020, https://dictionary.cambridge.org/dictionary/english/truth.

76 "Truth," Merriam-Webster, accessed on May 10, 2020, https://www.merriam-webster.com/dictionary/truth.

77 John MacArthur, *The Truth War: Fighting for Certainty in an Age of Deception* (Nashville, TN: Thomas Nelson, 2007), 2-4.

78 "Westminster Shorter Catechism - Q4," Bible Presbyterian Church General Synod, re-accessed April 1, 2022, https://bpc.org/?page_id=341. "God is a Spirit, infinite, eternal, and unchangeable, in his being, wisdom, power, holiness, justice, goodness, and <u>truth</u>" (emphasis added).

in John 14:6: The fact that anyone can come to God the Father only through Jesus Christ, the truth, means that God the Father Himself is also the truth. Meanwhile, in John 15:26, Jesus Christ said that the Holy Spirit, "the Spirit of truth," proceeded from God the Father. "The Spirit of truth" shows that the attribute and identity of the Holy Spirit is "truth" (genitive of apposition). God the Father, the Sender of the Holy Spirit, is also His Source in the functional hierarchy. Therefore, this eventually means that God the Father Himself, who sent the Holy Spirit, is also the 'truth' itself as the Source of truth.

The Second Person of the Holy Trinity: Truth as the Living Word of God

Jesus Christ, the second Person of the Holy Trinity as the Son of God, defines Himself as "the truth" in John 14:6: "I am the way, the truth, and the life: no man cometh unto the Father, but by me" (emphasis added). This means that to reach God who is 'truth,' it is only possible through Jesus Christ who is also "the truth." He also said in John 17:17, "Sanctify them through thy truth: thy word is truth." That is, in order to approach the holy God, the accessor must also be holy, and the process of sanctification for holiness can also be accomplished only by God's "truth." Jesus Christ additionally explains that "thy word," i.e. the Word of God, is "truth." Among the four Gospels, the Gospel of John focuses specifically on the Deity of Jesus Christ, and John 1:1-3 opens the preface to that book as follows: "In the beginning was the Word, and the Word was with God, and the Word was God. The same was in the beginning with God. All things were made by him; and without him was not any thing made that was made." Here, "the Word" refers to Jesus Christ, the second Person of the Holy Trinity. The phrases, "in the beginning was the Word" and "all things were made by him," are linked to וַיֹּאמֶר אֱלֹהִים ("And God said") that is repeated over and over at the scene of God's creation in the first chapter of Genesis. This reveals that the principle of God's creation, all things created by God's Word, is none other than the pre-incarnated Jesus Christ Himself: He is also the Creator. Putting it all together, the 'truth' of God who is 'truth' is His 'Word,' which is none other than Jesus Christ Himself. Therefore, Jesus Christ, the second Person of the Holy Trinity, is also 'truth' as the living Word of God.

The Third Person of the Holy Trinity: Truth as the Spirit of Truth

In the Bible, the Holy Spirit, the third Person of the Holy Trinity, is also repeatedly referred to as "the Spirit of truth." First and foremost, John 14:17 states that "the Spirit of truth" is the Holy Spirit who is indwelling only the saved. The Holy Spirit is also called "the Comforter" (John 15:26). Although He is essentially the very same God (Deut 6:4), He was sent by God the Father and God the Son in the functional hierarchy; and His role is to testify to Jesus Christ, who is 'the living Word of God' and 'the truth.' This role of "the Spirit of truth" is also evident in John 16:13: "the Spirit of truth, is come, he will guide you into all truth: for he shall not speak of himself; but whatsoever he shall hear, that shall he speak: and he will shew you things to come." That is, as "the Spirit of truth," the Holy Spirit was sent to guide people to Jesus Christ, "the truth" (Jn 14:6). Above all, apart from as the indwelling Spirit of the believers, the coming down of the Holy Spirit that Jesus Christ specifically promised before His ascension was the functional descent to preach the truth of the Gospel of Jesus Christ, the living Word, and to complete the written Word, which is filled with the truth of God. Accordingly, the completed written Word by the inspiration of the Holy Spirit is the 66 books of the holy Scriptures, the perfect Bible.

In this way, 'truth' is the God of the holy Trinity Himself, and the only means and output that God reveals His 'truth' is His 'Word.' And it is the Holy Spirit that leads the children of God into the 'truth' and makes them dwell in the 'truth.' This is the reason and ground for those who believe in God to worship Him "in spirit and in truth" (Jn 4:24[79]).

2.1.2 Features of Truth

The expression "truth" in the Bible uses אֱמֶת in the Old Testament and ἀλήθεια in the New Testament. The Hebrew word אֱמֶת corresponding to "truth" is used 127 times in 125 verses in the Old Testament,[80] and its meaning is divided into four categories as follows.[81]: (1) firmness, stability, perpetuity; (2) faithfulness, fidelity, truth (i.e. firmness and constancy in oneself, in keeping and executing one's promise, etc.); (3) truth (as opposite to falsehood); (4) good faith, uprightness, integrity. The root word of אֱמֶת, אָמַן, means "to believe" or "to be faithful," which connotes "to support" or "to be founded/firm/stable." Thus, through the Hebrew word אֱמֶת, the Old Testament describes "truth" in two complementary dimensions: "faithfulness" and "conformity to fact." In particular, "faithfulness" implied by אֱמֶת emphasizes on "the faithfulness of God"; "Conformity to fact" is a concept that encompasses "genuine, authentic, reliable" as well as God's wisdom and mercy related to all His laws and statues. In this regard, Nicole defined 'truth' as: "firm conformity to reality that proves to be wholly reliable, so that those who accept a statement may depend on it that it will not turn out to be false or deceitful."[82] Meanwhile, ἀλήθεια is used 110 times in a total of 99 verses in the New Testament,[83] and its meaning is defined in two broad categories as follows:[84] (1) objectively, the reality lying at the basis of an appearance; the manifested, veritable essence of a matter; (2) subjectively, truthfulness, truth, not merely verbal, but sincerity and integrity of character. The Greek word ἀλήθεια is equivalent to the Hebrew word אֱמֶת, but has a cognitive meaning that is emotionally more excluded than אֱמֶת; and etymologically stands for "being noticed by a correct perception of reality." Like אֱמֶת, ἀλήθεια also implies "faithfulness" or "conformity to fact," especially "conformity to reality" in terms of opposition against falsehood or error. In addition, beyond the

---

[79] "God is a Spirit: and they that worship him must worship him in spirit and in truth" (Jn 4:24)

[80] "H571," e-Sword desktop-based Bible software.

[81] Wilhelm Gesenius, *A Hebrew and English Lexicon of the Old Testament: Including the Biblical Chaldee* (Boston: Crocker and Brewster, 1859), 69.

[82] Roger Nicole, "The Biblical Concept of Truth," D. A. Carson and John D. Woodbridge, ed., *Scripture and Truth* (Grand Rapids, Michigan: Baker Book House, 1992), 288-292.

[83] "G225," e-Sword desktop-based Bible software.

[84] "225: ἀλήθεια," GreekLexicon.org, accessed on July 13, 2020, https://greeklexicon.org/lexicon/strongs/225.

dimensions of "faithfulness" or "conformity to fact," ἀλήθεια is also used to mean "completeness." Here, "completeness" is the fulfillment or complete realization of what God has said. Therefore, when the meanings of אֱמֶת and ἀλήθεια are combined, the biblical concept of "truth" includes "factuality, faithfulness, and completeness."[85]

Because God is truth, truth belongs to God's attributes, recalling the answer to Westminster Shorter Catechism Question No.4: "God is a Spirit, infinite, eternal, and unchangeable, in his being, wisdom, power, holiness, justice, goodness, and <u>truth</u>" (emphasis added).[86] In this definition, "truth" mentioned at the end is also one of the attributive domains, to which the aforementioned attributes of God ("a Spirit, infinite, eternal, and unchangeable") are applied. They are all interrelated: God is a Spirit in truth, infinite in truth, eternal in truth, and unchangeable in truth. Therefore, the truth of God, the truth itself, is endless and never changes.

In terms of those who deal with God's 'truth,' 'truth' is a concept that includes not only the quality of the propositions presented in a certain standard, but also living up to that standard. The Hebrew אֱמֶת corresponding to "truth" as reviewed earlier, also reflects the faithfulness of people to God's covenant in light of His faithfulness; And the Greek word ἀλήθεια also refers to "a person's integrity in speech, action, and thought."[87] Therefore, in order to live according to God's truth, it is necessary to understand what the truth is and what standards it has. God, of course, has the absolute standards of truth, morality, and ethics, and requires His people to obey them. And the truth of God and the standards in it remain unchanged; and the unchanging standard given to man to live according to the truth of God is "the Bible."[88] The Bible, the written Word of God, is the necessary and sufficient collection of truths given to man that Jesus Christ, the living Word of God, gave by the inspiration of the Holy Spirit. After God completed writing these 66 books of the Holy Scriptures, the full revelation of God's truth was also completed. The meaning of "completeness" connoted in the features of the truth is also applied to God's full revelation. The moment God's progressive partial revelation marked a period in the last verse of the last chapter of the Revelation, the full revelation had reached its necessary and sufficient state, and was complete. This is the perfect Bible given from God. Hence, after this perfect Bible, there has been no further revelation of God's truth, and the truth of God in this complete full revelation never changes. So, Timothy Tow has made mention of the Bible as "requires no new edition." He also said that the Bible is "the oldest book, yet ever new."[89] Here, "the oldest book" means God's completed full revelation, that is, His perfect Bible. Verbal Plenary Inspiration and Preservation, which have already been discussed in the earlier chapter, and 'the Law of

---

[85] Roger Nicole, "The Biblical Concept of Truth," 292-296.

[86] "Westminster Shorter Catechism - Q4," Bible Presbyterian Church General Synod, re-accessed July 13, 2020, https://bpc.org/?page_id=341.

[87] Gordon R. Lewis, *Testing Christianity's Truth Claims: Approaches to Christian Apologetics* (Chicago, Illinois: Moody Press, 1976), 20.

[88] John F. MacArthur, *Nothing but the Truth: Upholding the Gospel in a Doubting Age* (Wheaton, Illinois: Crossway Books, 1999), 63.

[89] Timothy Tow, *The Clock of the Sevenfold Will of God*, 69.

Inalterability,' which will be discussed immediately afterwards, are all about the core doctrines of this written Word: that is, about the principle and promise of, and the command for His perfect Bible, full of truth, that God has spoken.

2.2 The Law of Inalterability
2.2.1 Definition of the Law of Inalterability

The fact that God's Word never changes is what God has mentioned several times in the Bible: Matthew 5:18, which is already presented earlier, is a representative scriptural text for the fact that God's Word is preserved unchanged forever; Isaiah 40:8 says that even if the grass and flowers wither away, the Word of God will last forever; Matthew 24:35 and John 10:35 say that God's Word is "determined and fixed,"[90] so that it can never be damaged nor destroyed. In the same vein as Matthew 24:35, the Apostle Peter says in 1 Peter 1:23-25[91] that the Word of God they preached, the Gospel of Jesus Christ, is ever-present and always last forever. The same μένω is used for "abideth" of 1 Peter 1:23 and "endureth" of 1:25 in the Greek Scripture, and it contains the meaning of persistence, implying "to continue to be, not to perish, to last, to endure" in reference to time.[92] Moreover, both cases take the present tense, which emphasizes the present reality of the Word of God after it is uttered once (perfective present). God's written Word is the God-breathed Word which was penned through the human writers in accordance with the guidance of the Holy Spirit. This includes all the facts revealed before God beyond time and space, as well as what God spoke directly. God is the Creator, who has preserved His creations, and the perfect living Witness to human history. God directly declares that He is the beginning and end of history: "I am Alpha and Omega, the beginning and the end, the first and the last" (Rev 22:13). Thus, God's written Word is also God's testifying proclamation of the complete facts of human history, which men can never know completely. Because God transcends time and space, to God, even future events are historical facts that are already fulfilled. Then the moment God inspired and wrote the Word, all the facts recorded therein are God's utterances to proclaim to man. Thus, Burgon defines the Bible, the written Word of God, as "the direct utterance of the Most High."[93] In addition, both "abideth" in 1 Peter 1:23 and "endureth" in 1:25 are followed immediately by εἰς τὸν αἰῶνα to emphasize the ever-presence of the Word. This attribute of God's Word comes from the attribute of God, none other than its original Author. Westminster Shorter Catechism Question No. 4 answers the question "What is God?": "God is a Spirit, infinite, eternal, and unchangeable, in his being, wisdom, power,

---

[90] William W. Combs, "The Preservation of Scripture," *Detroit Baptist Seminary Journal* 5 (Fall 2000), 17.

[91] "Being born again, not of corruptible seed, but of incorruptible, by the word of God, which liveth and abideth for ever. For all flesh is as grass, and all the glory of man as the flower of grass. The grass withereth, and the flower thereof falleth away: But the word of the Lord endureth for ever. And this is the word which by the gospel is preached unto you" (1 Pet 1:23-25; emphasis added)

[92] "G3306," e-Sword desktop-based Bible software.

[93] "Dean Burgon Oath," ibid.

holiness, justice, goodness, and truth."[94] Among these attributes of God, there is 'unchangeableness,' and among the attributes that modify this 'unchangeableness,' "truth" of God is also included. This 'unchangeableness' of God is generally expressed in another other term 'immutability.' 'Immutable' comes from *"mutabills,"* which is derived from the Latin verb *"mutare* (to change)," and the negative prefix "in."[95] It carries the meaning of "unable to change," which is the same as "unchangeable" defined by Westminster Shorter Catechism. Therefore, according to God's immutable character, His "truth," or His Word, is also "unable to change." If God does not change, and if His Word cannot change according to His attributes, then there is no possibility that man can arbitrarily change His Word: for the Subject of its writing and preservation is God Himself, not man. Thus, Machen says this: "There are many things that change, but there is one thing that does not change. It is the Word of the living and true God. The world is in decadence, the visible Church is to a considerable extent apostate; but when God speaks we can trust him, and his Word stands forever sure."[96] Therefore, if this is considered together with the words of 1 Peter 1:23-25, the Word of God is ever-present and its 'unchangeability' is also permanent as well. Thus, The Apostle Paul gives a strict warning in Galatians 1:8-9 about the unchangeability of God's truth: "But though we, or an angel from heaven, preach any other gospel unto you than that which we have preached unto you, let him be accursed. As we said before, so say I now again, If any man preach any other gospel unto you than that ye have received, let him be accursed."

The writer specifically defines this unchangeable nature of God's Word as 'inalterability.' 'Immutability' and 'inalterability' are generally considered as interchangeable terms, but there are delicate differences. "Immutable" means "unable to be changed without exception," and "in(un)alterable" means "incapable of being altered; irrevocable or irreversible."[97,98] In the dictionary sense, "immutable" means "the state or quality of being immutable; not varying in different cases," which has to do with "without exception"; "Inalterable" is synonymous with "unalterable," also meaning "the quality of being inalterable."[99,100] That is, 'immutability' is more focused on the unchangeableness of a certain 'qualitative attribute,' and also implies the meaning of 'consistency' of that attribute; On the other hand, 'inalterability' suggests a more technical nuance that an object or system cannot be discarded, neither replaced, nor invalidated after it has been

---

[94] "Westminster Shorter Catechism - Q4," Bible Presbyterian Church General Synod, accessed July 07, 2020, https://bpc.org/?page_id=341.

[95] "Immutable," Merriam-Webster, accessed on June 25, 2020, https://www.merriam-webster.com/dictionary/immutability.

[96] J. Gresham Machen, *The Christian View of Man* (Carlisle, Pennsylvania: The Banner of Truth Trust, 1937), 14.

[97] "The difference between Immutable and Inalterable," DiffSense, accessed on June 26, 2020, https://diffsense.com/diff/immutable/inalterable.

[98] "Inalterable vs. Unalterable," AskDifference, accessed on April 12, 2022, https://www.askdifference.com/inalterable-vs-unalterable.

[99] *Shorter Oxford English Dictionary on Historical Principles: Volume 1·A-M*, 5th ed. (Oxford, U.K.: Oxford University Press, 2002), 1324, 1339.

[100] Noah Webster, *Webster's New Twentieth Century Dictionary*, unabridged 2nd ed., J. L. McKechine, ed. (Collins World, Cleveland: William Collins Publishers, Inc., 1979), 910, 919.

set up once. 'Immutability' is one of God's incommunicable attributes, while 'truth' is one of communicable intellectual attributes originating from God, whether men may or may not recognize it.[101] Then, under the providential permission of God and with the help of the Holy Spirit, it is not strange that there is a possibility for man to discover 'truth' from the Bible, the crystal of God's truth for man. However, this does not mean that man can replace or discard God's perfect written Word, which God has already completed once. This is because, as mentioned earlier, the Word of God is "determined and fixed."[102] In this respect, the writer prefers to use the term 'inalterability' rather than 'immutability' in relation to the human responsibility associated with the preservation issue of the perfect Bible.

Questions and controversies over whether the Bible is "the only Word of God" have continued with the history of the Bible. Among them, Verbal Plenary Preservation has also been the target of the most intense debates in relation to the Bible with Verbal Plenary Inspiration. Aside from those who don't believe that the Bible is the Word of God, even in the conservative camp that says they believe in the Bible as God's Word, most of them today seem to have turned their position to "No" against Verbal Plenary Preservation. While most of them still agree that 'the originals (autographs)' were written "by inspiration of God" (2 Tim 3:16), they question the fact that the written Word has still been preserved to this day. However, the preservation of God's Word is not determined by people's arguments. It is a direct promise given from God through His eternal Word (Mt 5:18; Ps 12:6-7; 1 Pet 1:23-25). Not only that, God also 'commands' man 'against' trying to alter the Word He Himself wrote and has preserved. This is because God has entrusted the responsibility of the archiving process to His faithful and true Church, i.e. the members of His true Church. There has always been God's true Church that seeks His truth, even in the fallen world and in the history of the sins that are raging. Although it is the visible local church on the earth that is always exposed to the possibility of corruption and apostasy, the militant true Church that sets themselves apart from the world and fights for the truth of the Lord has never disappeared in history:[103] for Jesus Christ Himself, the Head of the Church, is the Subject of the preservation. Thus, God, the original Author of the Word of truth and the Subject of preservation, has preserved His written Word to this day by using His true Church, which He has also preserved as His instrument. God also clearly stipulates what mode and attitude the

---

[101] M. E. Manton, *A Dictionary of Theological Terms* (London, U.K.: Grace Publications, 1996), 22-23.

[102] William W. Combs, ibid.

[103] Hyeonik Kwon, *The History of the True Church before the 16th-Century Reformation* (Seoul, Korea: Seum Books, 2019), 62-66. Taking Phillip Schaff, a protestant pastor as an example, the author of this book is keenly pointing out that Phillip Schaff distorted the history of the true Church because he was too faithful to the view of the history of the Roman Church. The representatively distorted claim is that the tradition of the Apostolic Church was cut off for a period of time, and then the history of the true Church was restored through the Reformation emerging in the arms of the Roman Church. In saying so, Phillip Schaff claimed that the Reformed Church had her roots in the Roman Church. This is the result of a thorough reliance on the history of the Roman Church, which has attempted to obliterate the history of the forerunner reformers before the Reformation from church history (pp.58-62). The problem is that this distorted history occupies most of the church history we can encounter today.

members of His true Church should take in dealing with God's written Word as the instrument of preservation. It is clearly commanded in God's law. Even today, God's promises regarding the preservation of the Word are still being kept perfectly. But the real question now is the mode and action of man toward the doctrine of Verbal Plenary Preservation, having derived all the evil consequences of deliberately violating God's law and commands regarding that doctrine and undermining the value of God's Word. Therefore, it is necessary to study the law and commands from the Bible that are required of man in relation to the preservation of the Word: That is 'the Law of Inalterability.' In addition, in light of 'the Law of Inalterability' enacted by God Himself, it is necessary to examine the status of people's actual mode and measure of dealing with His written Word.

2.2.2 The Law of Inalterability in the Bible: Consistency from the First to the Last Scriptures

The Bible is the Word of God comprised of 39 books of the Old Testament and 27 books of the New Testament. God not only promises to preserve His Word throughout the entire Bible, but also consistently commands the mode and attitude that the Church to whom God entrusted His Word should take toward it. In particular, in terms of God's 'written Word,' His command regarding the archiving of the Word is a strict warning against any arbitrary alteration of the Word, and is consistent throughout the entire Scriptures. And it starts with 'immutability,' the attribute of God Himself, the original Author of the Bible.

<u>God, the Author of the Scriptures, and the Inalterability of His Word</u>

God gave the Israelites the Ten Commandments through Moses for the first time after Exodus (Exod 20:1-17; Deut 5:1-22). But after that, Moses, furious at the golden calf incident of Aaron and the people who were waiting for him under Mount Sinai, broke the first stone tablets (Exod 32:19). Then, God once again commanded Moses to make two stone tablets identical to those that He Himself had made and given in the first place (Exod 32:16; 31:18; 24:12); and wrote the Ten Commandments a second time on the new tablets (Exod 34:1-9; Deut 10:1-5). These happenings related to the Ten Commandments speak of three important facts, all of which were directly revealed by God through His Word and His *de facto* measures regarding it.

First, it was God's own words handwritten by Himself. The Bible says twice that God gave the words engraved on the two tablets: The first was "two tables of testimony," which God gave to Moses on Mount Sinai for the first time after He had finished speaking (Exod 31:18); The second tablets were after Moses broke the first tablets (Exod 32:15-19) due to the golden calf incident of the Israelites. Then God once again gave Moses the two new tablets with the very same words (Exod 34:1- 9). Also, both the first and second tablets were handwritten by God Himself. The Hebrew Scripture of Exodus 31:18 records this as כְּתֻבִים בְּאֶצְבַּע אֱלֹהִים ("written with the finger of God"). As used herein, כָּתַב (kathab) is a verb meaning "inscribe" in addition to "write,"[104] and is used passively in Exodus 31:18. The preposition בְּ used in the prepositional phrase בְּאֶצְבַּע אֱלֹהִים ("with the finger of God") is an instrumental use of the "means, instrument, or mechanism." Therefore, they together express that God directly engraved His words on those stone tablets. Also, in Exodus 34:1 and Deuteronomy 10:2, God said that He would "inscribe" His words on the second tablets again ("I will write upon these tables," Exod 34:1b; Deut 10:2). All these facts very clearly show that the original Author of the Word is God Himself.

Second, God's Word is inalterable and identical. When God said to Moses "the words that were in the first table" (Exod 34:1b; Deut 10:2), the same commandments were engraved on the second tablets. In other words, it shows well that God's handwritten words remained the same even if the stone tablets changed. Something similar is recorded in Jeremiah 36. The evil king Jehoiakim burned all the words that God had made Baruch write through Jeremiah on the roll. However, God commanded Jeremiah again to have Baruch write on another roll with the very same words (Jer 36:28, "all the former words") that were on the first roll but had already been burned. In this way, God Himself protected and preserved His own words. One of God's attributes defined in Westminster Shorter Catechism's Question 4 is that He is "unchangeable." Since God's Word naturally follows God's attributes, it is sure and certain that His Word, the wisdom and the truth, is also "unchangeable" along with His other attributes. This is also well described in the answer to Question 4.[105] Therefore, even though the frame of God's Word may change, the Word of God itself, all the contents contained therein, is confirmed at the moment once uttered from the mouth of God and can never be changed.

Third, it is God who directly wrote the unchanging Word, and He must preserve His own Word for Himself. Nevertheless, it is man who is responsible for keeping the Word God has given him. When Moses broke the first tablets, God commanded Moses 'himself,' the attributable party, to make again and prepare the new stone tablets ("Hew thee two tables of stone like unto the first," Exod 34:1a; Deut 10:1). Then, when Moses made two new tablets of stone as God had made before, God again wrote the very same words on them. This implies 'human responsibility' for how to store and keep the God-given Word. In other words, the Preserver of the Word is God Himself (Divine Sovereignty: 'Verbal Plenary Preservation'), but there are certain things required of men as His chosen instruments for its preservation (Human Responsibility: 'The Law of Inalterability'). Interestingly, when making the second stone tablets, God also instructed Moses to make the ark to store the two stone tablets together inside (Deut 10:1-5). In other words, this means that not only man has the responsibility to store and keep the Word given from God, but also that the way of storage must be done in God's way. This is the context of 'the Law of Inalterability' to be discussed in the following section.

---

[104] "H3789," e-Sword desktop-based Bible software.

[105] "Westminster Shorter Catechism - Q4," Bible Presbyterian Church General Synod, re-accessed July 07, 2020, ibid. Westminster Shorter Catechism Answer 4 is this: "God is a Spirit, infinite, eternal, and <u>unchangeable</u>, in his being, wisdom, power, holiness, justice, goodness, and <u>truth</u>." (<u>emphasis added</u>)

<u>The Law of Inalterability in the Bible and Its Consistency</u>

Aside from God's handwriting of the Ten Commandments directly on the two table stones, God used human writers to pen all Scriptures. In Ephesians 2:20, the Apostle Paul speaks of the Church of Jesus Christ as those who are "built upon the foundation of the apostles and prophets, Jesus Christ himself being the chief corner stone." Here, "prophets" represent the Old Testament and "apostles" the New Testament; and God used them (prophets and apostles) as His instruments for the penning of His Word. Although God used them as the instruments for writing, the original Author is of course still God Himself. 2 Timothy 3:16 says, "All scripture is given by inspiration of God," and the Apostle Peter also affirms that all Scripture was spoken and written thoroughly by the Holy Spirit, not by any personal thoughts of the human writers. ("as they were moved by the Holy Ghost," 2 Pet 1:20-21). All these verses clearly state the fact that the original Author of the Bible is none other than 'God Himself.' Therefore, this fact also provides clear instruction to man who has been given the responsibility as God's instrument to share, keep, and even pass on His Word. It is 'the Law of Inalterability' concerning God's Word that no man can tamper with or replace the Word that God wrote, unless the original Author God Himself changes it. What is evident here is that God firmly nailed down to the fact that there would be 'no change' in His Word. Matthew 5:18 and 1 Peter 1:25 show God's sure and certain promise that even the smallest element in His Word will last forever. Therefore, 'the Law of Inalterability' is confirmed through His Word itself: man cannot arbitrarily change (not add, nor subtract, nor alter, nor replace) any of God's words once written. And God also clearly and severely wrote in His Word that 'the Law of Inalterability' applies equally throughout the whole of the Scriptures – from the first to the last.

From the First Scriptures: Deuteronomy 4:2 and 12:32 (13:1)[106]

The Five Books of Moses are God's first 'written' Scriptures out of a total of 66 books, and the Jews call it "Torah תּוֹרָה" ("Law"). "Torah תּוֹרָה" is also called "Pentateuch," which is a combination of the Greek words πέντε (five) and τεῦχος (scroll, book). Although in the modern sense it consists of five independent and self-contained books (Genesis, Exodus, Leviticus, Numbers, and Deuteronomy), "Torah תּוֹרָה" is not actually the collection of five "books" but a single "book." This is also confirmed by the fact that the Jews call "Torah תּוֹרָה" as "the five-fifths of the law," and "Pentateuch" also means "five-volumed (book)." It is also in the same context that when the Five Books of Moses are mentioned in the Bible, it is always used in the singular as "the <u>book</u> of Moses" or "the <u>law</u> of Moses." Thus, these Five Books are "purposefully structured and intended as part of a large unity." Also, in some sense, "Torah תּוֹרָה" can be regarded as the most important division of the Jewish canon with authority and sanctity

---

[106] Deuteronomy 12:32 is recorded as 13:1 in the original Hebrew Scripture.

that surpasses "Nevi'im נְבִיאִים" ("Prophets") and "Ketuvim כְּתוּבִים" ("Writings"):[107] for it is the base underlying the other two divisions of the Old Testament ("Prophets" and "Writings"). At the same time, it is constantly mentioned and cited in both the Old and New Testaments. In addition, "Torah תּוֹרָה" is the very first Scripture that God gave to man through Moses.

Deuteronomy, of "Torah תּוֹרָה" which is the first Scripture as a single book, is the book recorded by Moses, its human writer, just before his death; It is also the last subdivision of "Torah תּוֹרָה." Therefore, Deuteronomy is the book that commands the obedience to God's law while closing the first book of God's 'written' Word and looking forward the future things. In 'that' Deuteronomy 4:2, God commands His people through Moses, to obey His Word as follows:

לֹא תֹסִפוּ עַל־הַדָּבָר אֲשֶׁר אָנֹכִי מְצַוֶּה אֶתְכֶם וְלֹא תִגְרְעוּ מִמֶּנּוּ לִשְׁמֹר אֶת־מִצְוֹת יְהוָה אֱלֹהֵיכֶם אֲשֶׁר אָנֹכִי מְצַוֶּה אֶתְכֶם

> Ye shall not add unto the word which I command you, neither shall ye diminish ought from it, that ye may keep the commandments of the LORD your God which I command you.

Here, לֹא תֹסִפוּ ("shall not add") and לֹא תִגְרְעוּ ("neither shall… diminish") are commonly used in imperfect form with לֹא. The imperfect form with לֹא or the second-person jussive with אַל is used for a negative command to represent prohibition in Hebrew. Among them, the imperfect form used with לֹא is translated as "shall not," which stands for "a permanent, absolute prohibition." On the other hand, a jussive with אַל is a negative command applied to any immediate and specific situation that is not permanent, being translated as "do not."[108,109] In other words, compared to a jussive with אַל, the imperfect form with לֹא is used to express a very strong and absolute command with no exceptions allowed. Thus, the Hebrew negative commands used in Deuteronomy 4:2 indicates that what God forbids is an absolute command that can never be taken back, and no exception is allowed. This same strong command is repeated once again in Deuteronomy 12:32:

אֵת כָּל־הַדָּבָר אֲשֶׁר אָנֹכִי מְצַוֶּה אֶתְכֶם אֹתוֹ תִשְׁמְרוּ לַעֲשׂוֹת לֹא־תֹסֵף עָלָיו וְלֹא תִגְרַע מִמֶּנּוּ׃

> What thing soever I command you, observe to do it: thou shalt not add thereto, nor diminish from it.

In the Hebrew Scriptures for Deuteronomy 12:32 (13:1 in the original Hebrew text), the sentence corresponding to the first "observe to do it" has its object, אֹתוֹ ("it"), which is inverted and placed at the head of the sentence: This is an emphasis. Here, אֹתוֹ ("it") is the apposition אֵת כָּל־הַדָּבָר אֲשֶׁר אָנֹכִי מְצַוֶּה אֶתְכֶם ("What thing soever I command you"), which is another purpose clause presented immediately before אֹתוֹ ("it"). This is

---

[107] William S. Lasor, David A. Hubbard, and Frederic W. Bush, *Old Testament Survey: The Message, Form, and Background of the Old Testament* (Grand Rapids, Michigan: William B. Eerdmans Publishing Company, 1982), 54.

[108] Edwin C. Hostetter, *An Elementary Grammar of Biblical Hebrew* (England: Sheffield Academic Press, 2000), 70.

[109] Robert Ray Ellis, *Learning to Read Biblical Hebrew: An Introductory Grammar* (Waco, Texas: Baylor University Press, 2006), 182.

an expression to emphasize that God's ultimate emphasis is on 'all His words.' And תִּשְׁמְרוּ ("observe") is used in the imperfect, not imperative, which is the "injunctive imperfect" that represents a stronger forceful command than the jussive or the imperative. [110] Therefore, "observe to do it" here means "you <u>must</u> observe to do it." Also, the Hebrew verbs used for "keep" and "observe" in Deuteronomy 4:2 and 12:32 are both שָׁמַר (shamar), and שָׁמַר (shamar) has the meaning of "have charge of, guard, protect" in addition to "keep" and "observe."[111] Furthermore, "to do" connotes that 'obeying God's law' includes not only the meaning of 'knowing and understanding God's law merely with one's head,' but also of 'human responsibility to apply and practice it in real life.' After commanding obedience to and the practice of the Word, God uses "an absolute or permanent prohibition" once again by saying לֹא־תֹסֵף עָלָיו וְלֹא תִגְרַע מִמֶּנּוּ ("thou shalt not add thereto, nor diminish from it"), as in Deuteronomy 4:2. Here, the object "it" refers to אֵת כָּל־הַדָּבָר אֲשֶׁר אָנֹכִי מְצַוֶּה אֶתְכֶם ("What thing soever I command you") in the same way as the first command clause of the same verse. In other words, after stressing that His people must "observe" every command He gives, God is sternly warning that they can 'never' arbitrarily alter 'the' command.

The repetition of the same command in the Bible signifies an emphasis on its importance. In other words, giving man His first written Word through Moses, God confirmed and reaffirmed from the very first what mode and attitude man should take toward His Word. By using the expression "shall not," God assures that all commands He gives are fixed and permanent, so no one dares to touch them. In other words, from His first 'written' Bible given to man, God clearly reveals 'the Law of Inalterability,' that 'no man' can alter His Word 'forever.' This is God's powerful declaration and severe warning that man's arbitrary alteration of God's Word is never permitted.

Until the Last Scripture: Revelation 22:18-19

The book of Revelation, which was written by the Apostle John, is the last of the 27 books of the New Testament and the final book to complete the entire 66 canonical books of God's 'written' Word. Nay more, it is "the only book of the New Testament that is completely devoted to prophecy."[112] The Book of Revelation, prophesying about the second coming, judgment, and eternal kingdom of the Lord Jesus Christ, is the book that completely closes from the creation of this earthly world to its extinction, according to God's eternal decree from eternity past; At the same time, it is also the book that heralds the entry into the eternal life and blessings without sin. This final record of God, closing the last chapter of that last written Word of God, also ends up with a very serious and stern warning against the arbitrary alteration of His Word, as in Deuteronomy 4:2 and 12:32:

---

[110] Ronald J. Williams, *Williams' Hebrew Syntax*, 72.

[111] "Deuteronomy 12:32 - H8104," *Textus Receptus* Bibles, accessed on July 8, 2020, http://www.textusreceptusbibles.com/Strongs/5012032/H8104.

[112] Merrill C. Tenney, *New Testament Survey*, rev. Walter M. Dunnett (Grand Rapids, Michigan: WM. B. Eerdmans publishing Company, 1985), 381.

18
Συμμαρτυροῦμαι γὰρ παντὶ ἀκούοντι τοὺς λόγους τῆς προφητείας
τοῦ βιβλίου τούτου, Ἐάν τις ἐπιτιθῇ πρὸς ταῦτά, ἐπιθήσει ὁ Θεὸς
ἐπ' αὐτὸν τὰς πληγὰς τὰς γεγραμμένας ἐν βιβλίῳ τούτῳ·
For I testify unto every man that heareth the words of the prophecy of this book,
If any man shall add unto these things, God shall add unto him the plagues that are
written in this book:

19
καὶ ἐάν τις ἀφαιρῇ ἀπὸ τῶν λόγων βίβλου τῆς προφητείας ταύτης,
ἀφαιρήσει ὁ Θεὸς τὸ μέρος αὐτοῦ ἀπὸ βίβλου τῆς ζωῆς,
καὶ ἐκ τῆς πόλεως τῆς ἁγίας, καὶ τῶν γεγραμμένων ἐν βιβλίῳ τούτῳ.
And if any man shall take away from the words of the book of this prophecy,
God shall take away his part out of the book of life, and out of the holy city,
and from the things which are written in this book.

Revelation 22:18-19 strictly warns that no man can arbitrarily and indiscreetly "add unto" or "take away from" the complete written Word of God. Not just stopping at the warning, but taking one step further from Deuteronomy 4:2 and 12:32, Revelation 22:18-19 accompanies the merciless and unsparing consequences (God's eternal punishments) to those who have recklessly tried to alter the Word of God. In the Greek Scriptures of Revelation 22:18-19, the 3rd class condition (combining ἐάν with subjunctive in protasis) is used. This is also called the 'future condition,' which is a conditional clause based on 'fact,' for cases where the contents described in protasis have the potential to become reality.[113] In particular, the 3rd class (future) condition assumes the situation of "more probable future."[114] Therefore, it is such a structure that, if the condition described in protasis has a relatively high feasibility, and if the condition is satisfied, the contents described in apodosis are also realized together. When reviewing Revelation 22:18-19 in accordance with this grammatical structure, the object to watch out for in these verses is "the words of the prophecy of this book" (v.18; "the words of the book of this prophecy," v.19); And those conditions are God's terrifying warnings against any reckless alteration of His written Word, which was fully completed in Revelation 22. That is to say, God issues a prior warning that His completed written Word is the perfect and fixed Word which can no longer be changed; and therefore, no one can "add unto" or "take away from" that Word with one's arbitrary thoughts. These warnings of God presuppose the highly probable 'fact' that sinful men will do, and thus also warn the obvious 'fact' that God will surely punish them who dare to make such attempts. Moreover, the punishments not only include adding to them all the plagues recorded in the completed written Word, but also depriving eternal life from them. This means God's eternal punishments. Thus, according to Revelation 22:18-19, it is evident and sure that those who dare to alter the Word of God in spite of this unequivocal warning are unbelievers. As completing the full version of His 'written' Word, God warns and

---

[113] Jeffery Khoo, *Greek Exegesis I: Lecture Note* (Singapore: Far Eastern Bible College, 2019), 6.
[114] Daniel B. Wallace and Grant G. Edwards, *New Testament Syntax* (Grand Rapids, Michigan: Zondervan, 2007), 181.

reminds those unbelievers (who do not believe in His Word nor obey it) to see how serious it is to alter His Word according to their thoughts and judgment. Jesus Christ also says in John 10:27-28 and 14:23-24:

> "My sheep hear my voice, and I know them, and they follow me: And I give unto them eternal life; and they shall never perish, neither shall any man pluck them out of my hand." (Jn 10:27-28)
> "If a man love me, he will keep my words: and my Father will love him, and we will come unto him, and make our abode with him. He that loveth me not keepeth not my sayings: and the word which ye hear is not mine, but the Father's which sent me." (Jn 14:23-24)

God's children, chosen by Him according to His eternal decree from eternity past, must love the living truth, Jesus Christ, and heed His Word. The completed written Word of God, the 66 canonical books of the Scriptures, was given by Jesus Christ, the only perfect Shepherd. Thus, as those who have already been saved and enjoying eternal life, God's children must be bound to love the perfect Bible, which their heavenly Father has given necessarily and sufficiently for them. God's children always obey the Word, and will not dare to doubt or criticize it. Since it is the Word from God, His true children keep and entirely trust it, and just say "Amen."

In this way, as in the first Scripture, God proclaims 'the Law of Inalterability' in the last Scripture too. The beginning and the end of the entire Bible begin and end with the same warning from God, 'the Law of Inalterability': This is the same as the seal of God. This is a clear imprint that 'the Law of Inalterability' is God's will, His absolute warning and command that cannot be changed, and must be consistently applied throughout the Bible. Therefore, 'the Law of Inalterability' shows very clearly what mode and attitude man should take in dealing with the whole 'written' Word of God, the Bible.

2.2.3 Verbal Plenary Preservation, the Law of Inalterability, and Modern Validity

<u>Verbal Plenary Preservation and the Law of Inalterability:</u>
<u>Divine Authority and Human Responsibility</u>

Verbal Plenary Preservation is based on Verbal Plenary Inspiration, and Verbal Plenary Inspiration is guaranteed to be valid to this day through Verbal Plenary Preservation. One of the major premises of Verbal Plenary Preservation is that the original texts (autograph) have been preserved providentially <u>without any loss or alteration</u> through the manuscript copies (apograph).[115,116] Although God used human writers as the instruments for the penning of His Word, He inspired His 'Word' itself which was penned by them (2 Tim 3:16): that is, the direct Utterer and the original Author of the Word is God Himself, who never changes. Since God Himself is the absolute truth itself, He cannot have any loss nor alteration. Therefore, the Word that was written and

---

[115] "ABBREVIATIONS & DEFINITIONS," The Dean Burgon Society, accessed on March 30, 2020, http://deanburgonsociety.org/Preservation/miracle.htm.
[116] Young Gil Shin, 2.

has been preserved by God is also impossible for loss or alteration. This, of course, stems from immutability, one of God's attributes, which is already reviewed earlier.

The immutable God and His inalterable Word are also applied to the preservation process of the Word. God has been using His faithful and true Church as the instrument for the preservation of the Word, asking her to keep and pass down His Word He proclaimed and wrote, with full of fear and trembling. There is, of course, no authority given to His Church to attempt any alteration to the God-given Word; And of course, any thoughts or opinions of man, which are not spoken by God, cannot be added to God's Word either. Since the Church is the body of Jesus Christ, she only responds correctly according to the signals of Jesus Christ, the living Word as well as her Head, and His perfect, necessary, and sufficient written Word. If the body incorrectly reacts to the signals of its head, something is already wrong with it. But the true Church of Jesus Christ can never fail nor be destroyed. In the historical sense, true churches on earth can sometimes fail and fall in the tests, but that fact does not lead them to final destruction:[117] for God purifies His true churches (on earth) by purging them to reach His holiness. Therefore, the true Church of Jesus Christ ultimately heads in the direction of obedience to 'the Law of Inalterability.' Even when, for a moment, the members of His true churches fall in their weakness and fail to fully obey the command, the Word of God is preserved without any loss or alteration, because God raises up other true and faithful servants to defend His Word. Even when everyone fails, God's Word can never be changed, because the Subject of the preservation is God Himself, not man, and Verbal Plenary Preservation is God's own promise. Numbers 23:19 says: "God is not a man, that he should lie; neither the son of man, that he should repent: hath he said, and shall he not do it? or hath he spoken, and shall he not make it good?" Also, 1 Samuel 15:29[118] emphasizes that God cannot lie nor regret. Here, the Hebrew imperfect verb יִנָּחֵם corresponding to "repent" is used with a negative particle לֹא, which expresses a 'general truth'[119] that is always established regardless of time, and that God never reverse what He has decided, unlike human beings that change easily. In addition, the Hebrew word נֵצַח, corresponding to "the Strength" which expresses God, means not only "strength" but also "perpetuity, enduring, victory, and everlastingness."[120] That is, God's will that is once determined never fails, and its immutability implies that its effect is permanent. Because God is 'truth,' He cannot utter nor promise anything that contradicts His own attributes. Therefore, once God makes a promise with or an oath to His people, it is impossible for Him to break it Himself.[121]

---

[117] Hyeonik Kwon, *The History of the Ture Church before the 16th-Century Reformation*, ibid.

[118] "And also the Strength of Israel will not lie nor repent: for he is not a man, that he should repent" (1Sam 15:29)

[119] Wilhelm Gesenius, *Gesenius' Hebrew Grammar*, trans. from the 11th German edition by T. J. Conant, ed. (Boston: Gould, Kendall, and Lincoln, 1839), 249.

[120] "1 Samuel 15:29 - H5331," Textus Receptus Bibles, accessed on July 08, 2020, http://www.textusreceptusbibles.com/Strongs/9015029/H5331.

[121] It should be reminded that in the Bible, God's promise or covenant is always referred to God Himself. Since there is no one higher than God, God has sworn to Himself (Gen 22:16; Jer 22:5; 49:13). Also, "as I live, saith the LORD" is in the same vein. Since God is eternal and immutable, His promise or

There are countless instances in the Bible where God reveals the immutability of His Word and the faithfulness of His promises. It is expressed in a straightforward way of Divine preservation as in Matthew 5:18, but in some places, the authenticity of God's Word is emphasized using literary techniques. For example, in Jeremiah 1:11-12,[122] God gave Jeremiah a prophecy that He would discipline His people through the Babylonian Empire in the north because of the fall of the Southern Kingdom of Judah. The Hebrew word used for "an almond tree" in verse 11 is שָׁקֵד (shaqed), derived from שָׁקַד (shaqad) that is the original form of the participle verb שֹׁקֵד (shoqed) in verse 12 immediately following. Here, the meaning of the verb שָׁקַד (shaqad) is "watch," which means God emphasizes to Jeremiah the certainty of the fulfillment of His Word ("I will hasten my word to perform it") by engaging similar sounds of two words with the same roots,[123] as a form of word play. As such, the Word of God is firm and unchanging, so what remains to be demanded is the responsibility of man whom God has entrusted with His Word. Man's right mode and attitude toward the Word that has been preserved faithfully by God Himself is only to "keep" (Deut 4:2) and to "observe to do it" (Deut 12:32). As already reviewed in the Hebrew texts of Deuteronomy 4:2 and 12:32, the emphasizing point of 'the Law of Inalterability' is placed on 'all the Word of God'; and it is not simply to stop at the level of 'not changing any word of God,' but rather involves actively knowing, understanding, and obeying every word of God. This is 'human responsibility.' Obedience to 'the' command includes not only words, but all the choices and actions taken in life, from that which is trivial to that which is very important. One example of this is Moses' failure as found in Numbers 20:7-13. When the Israelites argued with Moses on the issue of water shortages, God planned to use Moses to supply them with water. In verse 8, what God commanded Moses was to "take the rod" and "speak ye unto the rock": "the rod" taken by Moses was to remind them of many of the miracles God had performed for the Israelites, and to let them have the confident assurance about their future. And all Moses had to do was just "speak" to the rock in front of the Israelites as God commanded him in verses 7-8. Then water would come out of the rock according to God's command spoken through Moses. However, even though Moses eventually caused water to come out of the rock, in that process, Moses did not obey what God had said to him to do, but disobeyed it by his action. God commanded Moses to simply "speak" toward the rock in order to make water come out of it, but Moses did something different that God did not command: hitting the rock twice with "the rod." Calvin points out that this is because Moses turned his eyes to the sins of the Israelites and failed to simply focus on the command God gave him. As a result, he did not fully trust in the word of

---

oath is also eternal and unchanging (Deut 32:39-40; Isa 49:18; Jer 22:24; 46:18; Ezek 5:11; 14:16, 18; 16:48; 17:16, 19; 18:3; 20:3, 31, 33; 33:11, 27; 35:6, 11; Zep 2:9).

[122] "Moreover the word of the LORD came unto me, saying, Jeremiah, what seest thou? And I said, I see a rod of an almond tree. Then said the LORD unto me, Thou hast well seen: for I will hasten my word to perform it" (Jer 1:11-12)

[123] E. P. Clowney. *Preaching Christ in All Scriptures* (Wheaton, Illinois: Crossway Books, 2003), 21-22.

God's promise based on God's grace and His power, but rather became to deny them.[124] It was the act of Moses that failed to completely obey God. As a result, Moses and Aaron were punished: They were not allowed to enter into Canaan, the promised land where they so desired (Num 20:23-24; 27:12-14). As such, the contents and importance of God's Word is not something that can be diluted or altered according to the consideration of the surrounding circumstances. The Word of God should not be disobeyed in any circumstance by any trivial word or small action. God only requires His people to obey His commands fully and completely from their hearts. Any attempt to recklessly alter the Word according to man's thoughts and intention is serious disobedience to God's command. This is the principle of 'Divine Authority' (Verbal Plenary Preservation) and 'Human Responsibility' (the Law of Inalterability) related to the Word of God that never changes, and these two are connected to each other.

'The Law of Inalterability' of God's Word is the law that is consistently applied to the entire Bible, and at the same time, is the stern and severe warning given to men who are used by God as His instruments in the process of preserving the Word. Therefore, 'the Law of Inalterability' must be applied equally to the believers living in modern times. For this reason, it is significant and meaningful to check the real status of this human responsibility for this law today. Verbal Plenary Preservation is the sure and certain promise on the part of God, but on the part of man, it is a matter of mode, attitude and practical measure in dealing with the Word that God is still preserving. Today, however, too many Bible versions being supplied to and used by the believers are distorted apart from God's authentic written Word, which He originally wrote and has preserved. And this distortion stems from the corruption of the manuscripts (and thus, the texts) that underlie those translations. Moreover, the believers are misled by the claim that the corrupted manuscripts should be more academically superior and acceptable. It is rooted in the deliberate overlook of and the lack of accountability for the strict commands and warnings God has already made clear in His Word. It is the pride of man which encompasses all those problems. The unbelief in Verbal Plenary Preservation today and all the debates that are derived from it are due to the mode and attitude, which the people are taking towards God's Word, inconsistent with God's command. In other words, all these problems originate from the defiance of and disobedience to 'the Law of Inalterability,' which God commands man for the whole Word. And, in fact, the problem began to take root from Satan's deliberate distortion of God's words towards man whom God created.

Defiance to the Law of Inalterability: The Subtle and Sinful Plot

In Genesis 2:16-17, God gave Adam, the first man, a prohibition order related to the fruits "of the tree of the knowledge of good and evil." This was a test under 'the Covenant of Works' that was given when man was still under God's probation before he sinned. In other words, by voluntarily choosing obedience to God's command with God-

---

[124] John Calvin, *Commentaries on the Four Last Books of Moses Arranged in the Form of a Harmony* (Grand Rapids, Michigan: Baker Book House, 1984), 133-135.

given free will of his own, he could acquire his eternal sonship and enter into eternal life that would also be given to him by God. In Genesis 2:17, the same as in Deuteronomy 4:2 and 12:32, 'an absolute or permanent prohibition' is also used for the prohibition of eating the fruits "of the tree of the knowledge of good and evil" ("shall not eat"). And in the same verse, "shall surely die" as a result of disobedience to the command is not only a prohibition, but also an emphasis in the form of 'double death' (מוֹת תָּמוּת in Hebrew; literally, "dying thou shalt die," "thou shalt surely die").[125] In other words, God repeatedly emphasized that the result of disobedience to His prohibition order must be death. However, in Genesis 3:1-5, Satan began his deliberate distortion by questioning God's Word with doubt when seducing the woman. Satan's cunning distortion of God's Word and the woman's false reaction to it, that is, the alteration of God's Word can be compared as below:

God's Commandment (Gen 2:16-17)	Satan's distortion/Woman's Alteration (Gen 3:1-5)

▪ *"Of every tree of the garden thou mayest freely eat"* (v.16)
  ‣ Including the tree of life; except the tree of the knowledge of good and evil
	▪ Satan's doubtful and distortive questioning: *"Yea, hath God said, Ye shall not eat of every tree of the garden?"* (v.1)
	  ‣ Deliberate question to induce distortion: including the tree of the knowledge of good and evil
	▪ Woman's response: *"We may eat of the fruit of the trees of the garden"* (v.2)

▪ *"of the tree of the knowledge of good and evil"* (v.17)
  ‣ The specified tree
	▪ Woman's subtraction: *"of the fruit of the tree which is in the midst of the garden"* (v.3)
	  ‣ Take out the specified word and lump together

▪ *"thou shalt not eat of it"* (v.17)
  ‣ An absolute or permanent prohibition
	▪ Woman's addition: *"Ye shall not eat of it, neither shall ye touch it"* (v.3)
	  ‣ Add a condition God has not spoken of

▪ *"thou shalt surely die"* (v.17)
  ‣ Double death in grammatical form: an emphasis on the certainty of the death penalty
	▪ Woman's alteration: *"lest ye die"* (v.3)
	  ‣ Change the tone (thus, meaning too)
	▪ Satan's reverse wording against God's command: *"Ye shall not surely die"* (v.4)
	  ‣ Change God's original command in a completely opposite sense
	▪ Satan's addition: *"your eyes shall be opened, and ye shall be as gods, knowing good and evil"* (v.5)
	  ‣ Add seducing words

The expression "subtil" used for Satan in Genesis 3:1 is evident in his craftiness to rebel against God's Word. The woman eventually got caught up in his intentional

---

[125] R. Laird Harris, *Introductory Hebrew Grammar* (Grand Rapids, Michigan: WM. B. Eerdmans Publishing Company, 1950), 30-31; Wilhelm Gesenius, *Gesenius' Hebrew Grammar*, 342. In Hebrew, the infinitive absolute used before the finite verb of the same stem emphasizes the verbal idea, indicating the certainty or completeness of its occurrence.

temptation, and as a result, made a fatal wrong choice that violated 'the Law of Inalterability' by adding, subtracting, and altering the words of God. Satan never missed this opportunity, ultimately leading the woman to a total denial of God's command. Note that the singular pronoun "thou" was used when God commanded Adam the prohibition order. However, when Satan seduced the woman, it was replaced by the plural pronoun "Ye." It means that Adam was also next to the woman when she was tempted, and that Satan's deliberate distortion of the words of God and the temptation through it were aimed not only at the woman but also at Adam.[126] This, in turn, suggests that the woman's choice of sin was made together with Adam's acquiescence.

As such, the subtle alteration of God's Word has a deep-rooted history inherent in the sinful nature of man, which began with the communication between Satan and the very first man who was created by God. Satan, of course, still has no thought of giving up that temptation. He twisted the words of God to test the first Adam; and also tempted Jesus Christ, the second and last Adam, using the Word of God (Mt 4:1-11; Mk 1:12-13; Lk 4:1-13). Impudently and recklessly, Satan arbitrarily interpreted (eisegesis) and even distorted the Word in front of Jesus Christ, the living Word Himself and the Author of the Word, and dared to use it to seduce Him. However, Jesus Christ overcame all the persistent temptations of Satan [127] through the right use of God's Word as it is. Nevertheless, Satan's temptation still continues today, and his target is always the Word of God: the written Word, the perfect Bible that God completed its writing and has preserved thus far. And Satan's final goal, as he did to the first Adam, is total denial of God's Word.

Verbal Plenary Preservation and the Law of Inalterability: Modern Validity

The Bible says that God always keeps the covenant with His faithful servants (1 King 8:23; Neh 9:32). And God's promise of preservation of the Word, Verbal Plenary Preservation, has been kept to this day through His faithful and true Church. The originals (autographs) of the 66 books have been preserved through faithfully-transcribed-and-thoroughly-verified copies (apographs). The Old Testament has been preserved so far through the 'Masoretic Text' (in Hebrew and partially in Aramaic) and the New Testament through the '*Textus Receptus*' (traditional, majority, and received text; in Greek). The continuity of Verbal Plenary Preservation through faithful and verified apographs is also the basis for the continuity of Verbal Plenary Inspiration, which is the principle of God's writing of the autographs. Therefore, Verbal Plenary Preservation is not the promise only applied when God wrote the Bible or at any certain time. For God

---

[126] This fact is clearly confirmed in the verse immediately following: "And when the woman saw that the tree was good for food, and that it was pleasant to the eyes, and a tree to be desired to make one wise, she took of the fruit thereof, and did eat, and gave <u>also unto her husband with her</u>; and he did eat" (Gen 3:6; <u>emphasis added</u>).

[127] In Matthew 1:13, the Greek verb for "tempted" is used in the present participle. The Greek present tense indicates a kind of 'continuous or repeated' action. In other words, it suggests that Satan continuously repeated his temptations recorded in Matthew 4:1-11 and Luke 4:1-13 throughout these 40 days Jesus was in the wilderness.

and the members of His faithful Church, Verbal Plenary Preservation is the promise of 'present progressive' meaning that is still being realized not only on the part of God as its Subject, but also the law ('the Law of Inalterability') to be kept on the part of man who has been given responsibility as His instrument to keep, store, and transmit the Word of God.

Critical Texts: The Arbitrary Alteration of God's Word

Today, however, many churches and theologians overlook or deliberately ignore 'the Law of Inalterability' and its human responsibility, which God commands directly through His Word. The reason is obvious: their unbelief in God, the Subject of the promise of Verbal Plenary Preservation prior to 'the Law of Inalterability.' Their unbelief in God naturally leads them to unbelief in His Word, so they evaluate Verbal Plenary Preservation not according to God's absolute truth, but according to man's standards: that is textual criticism, which relies heavily on human reason and so-called scientific methodology. Textual criticism is also overwhelmingly supported by the modern critics. Textual criticism, which aims to collect evidences from all available manuscripts and to reconstruct them as close as possible to the original texts, is also called as 'lower criticism.'[128] The reason the modern critics do this is because of the imperfections of their manuscripts. After the Apostolic era when the originals (of the 66 books of the written Word) were just completed by the completion of the 27 books of the New Testaments through the Apostles, their inaccurate and unreliable manuscripts also had existed such as the Alexandrian manuscripts.[129] However, the corrupted manuscripts were either spoiled or abandoned because of the quality of the errors they contained. This is in contrast to God's preservation of traditional/majority/received text (Byzantine text) through the Church, which is militant for truth on earth. Nevertheless, the modern critics, who had already concluded that Verbal Plenary Preservation was 'impossible,' were simply enthusiastic when 'new' (but corrupted) material, satisfying their so-called academic standards, came out. That is the revised text (1881) of Westcott and Hort, which was completed on the basis of the corrupted manuscripts which had been rejected by the Church before the 4th century. Instead of rigorously evaluating the authenticity of those manuscripts, whether they were truly of the originals or not from a biblical and ecclesial perspective, they 'opted' to advocate them just because they were older than the extant texts. However, their trust in the right apographs, which God has perfectly preserved

---

[128] Eldon Jay Epp and Gordon D. Fee, *Studies in the Theory and Method of New Testament Textual Criticism* (Grand Rapids, Michigan: William B. Eerdmans Publishing Company, 1993), 3.

[129] Colin D. Standish and Russell R. Standish, *The Perils of Ecumenism* (Rapidan, Virginia: Hartland Publications, 2003), 38-44. The Alexandrian School (Western), which exerted a strong influence on the Roman church, had an academic stance that looked at the Greek New Testament and Christianity from a perspective based on Plato god Greek philosophy, leading them to hold different theologies from the Antioch School (Eastern) and even to allow pagan infiltration. Thus, while the Antioch School just focused on preserving the originals without any arbitrary judgment or practice, the Alexandrian School made many arbitrary alterations in their copying process on the pretext of improving and correcting the writings of the New Testament. This is the Alexandrian manuscripts that have been the root of many codicological problems and controversies.

without any loss or error through His faithful and true churches, has been so easily abandoned. The critics' mode and attitude toward the Bible is not unrelated to the academic obsession with 'newness' based on 'Evidentialism'; And the obsession with 'newness' is closely related to the trend of the theological compromise about truth and faith in it. It is common for these academic trends to re-examine, revise, or further overturn or dispose of existing theories according to newly discovered evidences. Therefore, the critics were given an excuse for the justification to replace the traditional text, which had been properly kept, in line with the critical texts, only because the materials that suited their taste as well as met such academic demands were rediscovered. For that, the critics did not hesitate to justify the critical texts as being closer to the originals. Therefore, 'the Law of Inalterability' meant nothing to them. Since then, the critics (or now most theologians and pastors) have already made numerous arbitrary alterations to the Word of God at their discretion. It has long been forgotten in people's minds since 'what the right manuscript is' as well as 'the necessity of examining other materials according to the right manuscript' has been dismissed as outdated. Most theologians, as well as pastors and church members, no longer seek or respect the perfect Bible. What best reveals that fact is the constant revisions of the critical texts and the modern versions translated based on those texts. For example, since Eberhard Nestle published the first edition of his *Novum Testamentum Graece* ("Nestle-Aland") in 1898, it has been continually revised until the 28th edition came out in 2012. The "Nestle-Aland" was based on the readings of Tischendorf, Westcott and Hort, and Weymouth (later, Weymouth was replaced by the 1894/1900 edition of Bernhard Weiß), which were then the leading scholarly editions, but at the same time the critical texts. All the while, it has served as a vehicle for spreading textual criticism. On the other hand, starting with the 26th edition, the "Nestle-Aland" has been constantly revising its contents whenever any new materials were discovered, including the introduction of fundamentally new techniques, reflecting the newly discovered early papyri and other manuscripts. Thus, such continual revisions of the critical texts, of course, have had no choice but to influence on the English versions translated based on them. The modern translated versions based on the critical texts do not hesitate to arbitrarily translate even the words of God related to 'the Law of Inalterability' by replacing their original wording. For example, the King James Version faithfully translated Deuteronomy 4:2 as "shall not" as written in the original Hebrew text. However, the modern versions, such as the New International Version (NIV), the International Standard Version (ISV), or The Living Bible (TLB), have not only mitigated this phrase to "Do not," but also completely reconstructed the sentence structure of its original text as below in the table. In addition, the phrases that are not written in the original Hebrew text are also added to their translations. For example, The Living Bible (TLB) inserts "other laws" that are not found in the Hebrew

Scriptures, or replaces the third person singular male pronoun הוּ, which is combined with the preposition מִן, by the plural pronoun "these."[130] These are all paraphrasing:

Hebrew Original Scripture	לֹא תֹסִפוּ עַל־הַדָּבָר אֲשֶׁר אָנֹכִי מְצַוֶּה אֶתְכֶם וְלֹא תִגְרְעוּ מִמֶּנּוּ לִשְׁמֹר אֶת־מִצְוֹת יְהוָה אֱלֹהֵיכֶם אֲשֶׁר אָנֹכִי מְצַוֶּה אֶתְכֶם
King James Version	"Ye <u>shall not</u> add unto the word which I command you, <u>neither shall</u> ye diminish ought <u>from it</u>, that ye may keep the commandments of the LORD your God which I command you."
New International Version	"<u>Do not</u> add to what I command you and <u>do not</u> subtract from it, but keep the commands of the Lord your God that I give you." ‣ Changes in words and sentence structure
International Standard Version	"<u>Do not</u> add or subtract <u>a thing</u> to what I'm commanding you. Observe the commands of the Lord your God." ‣ Changes in words and sentence structure
The Living Bible	"<u>Do not</u> add <u>other laws</u> or subtract <u>from these</u>; just obey them, for they are from the Lord your God." ‣ Changes in words and sentence structure

(emphasis added)

These arbitrary alterations reduce the seriousness degree (absolute and permanent strong prohibition) of 'the Law of Inalterability,' which is applicable to the whole Bible, to the level of 'simple and temporary prohibition according to the situation' while diluting the clarity of the context. This is like creating 'words' in a completely new context, rather than God's original Word: for there is the obvious Divine reason not only for every word that God used when writing the Bible, but also for the composition and structure of the sentences in it. Therefore, the use of the critical texts that have added to or omitted from or modified in the original texts (meaning the traditional/ majority/received text) and thus already contain arbitrary alterations, and further, the arbitrary translations according to human judgment: all these are the collection of alterations that clearly violate 'the Law of Inalterability.' The problem is that most theologians and pastors today, who have to take on the responsibility of keeping the Word, are adopting the thinking system of the modern critics; Rather, it is considered as appropriate and rational to determine the authenticity of the Bible by man other than the Almighty God, the original Author and Preserver of the Bible. As such, today is a time when it is extremely rare for people to trust in Verbal Plenary Preservation and adhere to the mindset and mode of 'the Law of Inalterability' as God promised and commanded. However, rather paradoxically, it provides a clear reason why 'the Law of Inalterability,' regarding the mode and attitude of man who must come with a godly heart and sincere attitude to that responsibility as God's instrument to keep and defend the Word of God, should be more emphasized and maintained.

---

[130] Here, הוּ is a pronoun referring to הַדָּבָר, and since הַדָּבָר is a singular masculine noun in the Hebrew text, הוּ also has the same characteristic with הַדָּבָר. This arbitrary change to the plural form done by the Living Bible is because the immediately preceding phrase has also been arbitrarily paraphrased.

2.3 Errors from Overconfidence and Misrepresentation: Ruckmanism

"What and where are the preserved words of God today?" To this question related to Verbal Plenary Preservation, among the other doctrines she adheres to, Far Eastern Bible College answers as below:[131]

> The inspired OT Hebrew words and NT Greek words the prophets, the apostles, the church fathers, the reformers used which are today found in the long and continuously abiding and preserved words underlying the Reformation Bibles best represented by the time-tested and time-honoured KJV, and **NOT** in the corrupted Alexandrian manuscripts and critical Westcott-Hort texts underlying the liberal, ecumenical, and neo-evangelical modern English versions.

The Westminster Confession of Faith Chapter 1 Paragraph 8 also defines the Holy Scripture in the same context as Far Eastern Bible College does:[132]

> The Old Testament in Hebrew, (which was the native language of the people of God of old), and the New Testament in Greek, (which, at the time of the writing of it, was most generally known to the nations), being immediately inspired by God, and, by his singular care and providence, kept pure in all ages, are therefore authentical; so as, in all controversies of religion, the Church is finally to appeal unto them. But, because these original tongues are not known to all the people of God, who have right unto, and interest in the scriptures, and are commanded, in the fear of God, to read and search them, therefore they are to be translated into the vulgar language of every nation into which they come, that the word of God dwelling plentifully in all, they may worship him in an acceptable manner, and, through patience and comfort of the Scriptures, may have hope.

As commonly found in these statements, when the written Word of God is mentioned, it means the faithful 'traditional/majority/received' text that God wrote and has preserved to this day and still exists: the Masoretic Hebrew Scriptures for the Old Testament and the *Textus Receptus* Greek Scriptures for the New Testament. Thus, when considering the principles of writing and preservation of the Word that God has spoken through His Word, as well as the practical process and effectiveness of its preservation within the history of the true church, it is clear that the critical texts as well as the modern versions based thereon cannot be 'the' preserved written Word. Nevertheless, the modern critics have committed the sin of defying God's Word with intentional disregard for 'Verbal Plenary Preservation' and 'the Law of Inalterability' with excessive overconfidence in human reason. The critics, who use but do not obey the Word of God, are considered to be some sort of left-skewed extremists, who do not reach the Word due to their pride of so-called 'scholarship.' On the other hand, there are also right-skewed extremists, who misrepresent their overinterpretation of the Bible as the truth, beyond

---

[131] DOCTRINE/VERBAL PLENARY PRESERVATION, "THE VERBAL PLENARY PRESERATION OF THE SACRED SCRIPTURES," Far Eastern Bible College, accessed on July 10, 2020, https://www.febc.edu.sg/v15/article/verbal_plenary_preservation.

[132] "Westminster Confession of Faith Chapter 1: Of the Holy Scripture - no.8," Bible Presbyterian Church General Synod, re-accessed on March 22, 2020, ibid.

what God has said: that is Ruckmanism. As mentioned above, the inspired and preserved written Word is none other than the original texts written in common languages at that time when God performed the writing of His Word (the 'Hebrew' Old Testament and the 'Greek' New Testament). However, Ruckmanism has made the error of extending the doctrine of Verbal Plenary Inspiration (that is only applied to the above original texts) to a translated version based on them. Here, in order to understand Ruckmanism and its problematic seriousness, understanding the difference between 'text' and 'translation' must be preceded.

<u>Text versus Translation</u>

When some people refer to the written Word or the Bible, they are confused whether it is the Hebrew and Greek original texts or their translated versions. In addition, today, except for those who are interested in theology or the original biblical languages, it is understood to people that the Bible usually means the translations, not the original texts. Therefore, it is first necessary to define the terms related to Ruckmanism, before discussing its doctrinal errors. Here, the two most important things to distinguish are 'text' and 'translation.' According to Philip W. Comfort, 'text' is 'the original writings' in a word, and the original biblical texts are the original Scriptures written in Hebrew (Aramaic in part) and Greek. The original writings are again divided into "the autographs" and "manuscripts": "the autographs" means "the originals," that is, "actual writings of the Old Testament prophets and the New Testament apostles"; And "manuscripts" are also called "the apographs," which means "Hebrew and Greek copies." Here, "Hebrew and Greek copies" means the original Hebrew Old Testament copied into the same Hebrew and the original Greek New Testament into the same Greek.[133] Both sides, "the autograph" and "manuscripts," are sometimes referred to as "source texts" or "underlying texts" in comparison to 'translation,' which refer to the writings that convert these "underlying texts" into the native language of each target country. However, since "the autographs" of the Bible no longer exist today, their "manuscripts" (i.e. "the apographs") that copied them identically and accurately have been taking over the role of "underlying texts" instead of them (i.e. "the autographs").

Based on the definitions of 'text' and 'translation,' the next issue to be discussed in order to review Ruckmanism is Verbal Plenary Inspiration. In 2 Timothy 3:16, God has already made it clear that the principle of writing His Word is 'Divine inspiration.' And this was already accomplished by the Holy Spirit's supernatural work in the original texts ("the autographs").[134] And the copies of the original texts, not the corrupted but the received, have been preserved in the original languages rendered exactly and accurately. In such a copying process, only exact accuracy was required. Human thoughts or judgments were not allowed to be involved therein: for it is the purpose of the

---

[133] Philip W. Comfort, *Essential Guide to Bible Versions* (Wheaton, Illinois: Tyndale House Publishers, 2000), 99.

[134] David W. Cloud, *The Bible Version Question-Answer Database: Answering the Myths Promoted by Modern Version Defenders* (Port Huron, Michigan: Way of Life Literature, 2005), 161.

"manuscripts" of the Bible to render all the contents of the God-inspired originals ("the autographs") as they were in their original languages, without any addition, subtraction or alteration. In other words, the manuscripts ("the apographs") of the Bible must be the 'exactly identical duplicates' of their originals ("the autographs"). If not, the manuscripts were not simply copied from their originals into another document, but transformed into something other than God's original written Word through the intervention of a copyist's (or copyists') intentions. This is the arbitrary alteration God has sternly warned against (that is, against 'the Law of Inalterability'). Then, of course, such manuscripts can'not' be exactly accurate manuscripts ("the apographs") of God's original written Word ("the autographs"). Thus, in order for manuscripts ("the apographs") to be the subject of Divine preservation, the prerequisite of the 'exactly identical duplicates' must be met. Accordingly, Divine inspiration is applied only to 'those' manuscripts (the identical duplicates as "the apographs") to which every single word of the God-inspired originals was copied exactly and accurately. This is because, although human writers penned in accordance with the guidance of the Holy Spirit, the actual target of Divine inspiration was not those human writers, but all the written Word of God itself (2 Tim 3:16, πᾶσα γραφὴ θεόπνευστος, "All scripture *is* given by inspiration of God," emphasis added): the Old in Hebrew and the New in Greek.[135]

However, 'translation' is another matter. In the process of rendering the original texts into 'another' language, the translator's understanding of the original texts and their judgment and selection of proper words in the translation target language, which can be closest to the original meaning, are inevitably involved. Therefore, above all else, the translator must be very fluent in both languages: the original language to be translated and the target language to be rendered. Even if the above conditions are met, the translator must have a right and correct doctrinal basis and a sufficient historical, cultural and literary understanding of the original texts. Then there is methodology. There are two methods related to Bible translation: one is 'formal equivalence,' and the other is 'dynamic equivalence.' 'Formal equivalence' is also called 'word-for-word' or 'literal' translation, and in this technique, the translator's top priority lies in the output of the translation closest to the originals by reflecting the words most corresponding to the original meaning in translation. In contrast, 'dynamic equivalence,' which is known as 'thought-for-thought' or 'functional' translation, is to make the originals easy to be understood by and have an impact on readers, taking into account the historical and cultural gap between the original texts and modern readers.[136] In simple terms, 'formal equivalence' is a biblical translation methodology with its emphasis on the original text

---

[135] It was the Antioch School that just focused all their attention on completing the perfect 'identical duplicates' of all inspired words written in the originals; And the manuscripts completed by the Antioch School were the Byzantine Text, and the *Textus Receptus* that followed after the invention of the printing press. On the contrary, the Alexandrian School caused the production of the corrupted manuscripts by allowing the intervention of copyists and their arbitrary alterations resulting therefrom, based on human philosophies and thoughts. Thus, from their root, the extant critical texts already harboured the serious problem of disqualification as the identical duplicates of the originals.

[136] Philip W. Comfort, *Essential Guide to Bible Versions*, 103.

itself, but the emphasis of 'dynamic equivalence' is on readers, especially on their reaction. Therefore, in 'dynamic equivalence,' the focus of the translation has already shifted from 'text' itself to readers. However, the translation of the Bible must be done according to 'formal equivalency,' because it is not for human reaction but ultimately for the most accurate transmission of the Word of God in the target language. Even if the intervention of human judgment is essential in the translation process, the degree of intervention must be strictly restrained within the scope of sound and correct doctrines. This is to reduce the possibility of the translator's arbitrary judgment in the Bible translation process. However, beyond all these matters, even when these conditions are perfectly met, if the translator uses the wrong source text, the other process becomes meaningless. Therefore, the right 'translation' must start from the right 'text': i.e. the Hebrew Masoretic and the Greek *Textus Receptus*, the traditionally received texts that God has preserved to this day through His faithful and true churches. As already found from the methodological matter itself mentioned above, the work of 'translation' inevitably involves the judgment of its translator. Thus, it has nothing to do with the effect that the Holy Spirit had already inspired the Hebrew and Greek original words in the Scriptures when they were written, and only the matter of how faithful and accurate translation was/is performed by the translator remains in the translated.

<u>The Errors of Ruckmanism: Overconfidence and Misrepresentation</u>

There are so many English Bible translations today, but among others, the King James Version is "the best English translation of the Scriptures, made by godly translators from uncorrupted Hebrew and Greek texts."[137] This is especially because: 1) The King James Version is based on the thoroughly correct 'texts' (the Masoretic Hebrew Old Testament and the *Textus Receptus* Greek New Testament); 2) While its translators had the correct theology in relation to the biblical doctrines, they were also the well-versed scholars in Hebrew and Greek; 3) In the translation work, the arbitrary judgment of the translators was excluded; 4) Based on the Word-centered thinking and using the 'formal equivalency' technique, its translators even translated the grammatical usage of the original texts into English very delicately and accurately.[138] In terms of the most faithful and accurate reflection of the original texts, the King James Version has a superiority that surpasses the myriad other extant English Bible versions today; And that is why the King James Version has been dominant as the most faithful 'translation' to 'text,' even since the authorize version was published in 1611.

However, one thing that must NOT be forgotten is that 'translation' is 'translation.' In Bible translation, there is no 'translation' that is 100% perfectly equivalent to the inspired original texts. No matter how accurately and faithfully any Bible version is translated, it cannot be better than the original Hebrew and Greek texts

---

[137] Jeffrey Khoo, *KJV Questions & Answers* (Singapore: Bible Witness Literature Ministry, 2003), 8.

[138] D. A. Waite, *Defending the King James Bible* (Collingswood, New Jersey: The Bible for Today Press, 1996), 20-183.

themselves.[139] As a reminder, 'translation' inevitably involves the very careful judgment of the translator for the most exact and accurate translation possible in the process of rendering the original languages into other languages. Even if the best word in terms of accuracy and nuance is chosen at the discretion of the translator, it cannot be the originals themselves. Therefore, when any errors in translation are found or there are better translation alternatives, corrections are made to the translation. The King James Version was also completed in today's form after several major and minor edits.[140] However, 'texts,' especially the Hebrew Masoretic and the Greek *Textus Receptus* which God has preserved intact to this day, are "the apographs" that are equivalent to "the autographs," being thoroughly and faithfully received by the faithful and true churches of Jesus Christ: These 'texts' are the objects of God's inspiration and preservation.

Ruckmanism is an extreme form of "King James Onlyism," advocated by Peter Ruckman. "King James Onlyism" is a claim that only the King James Version is the Word of God which has been providentially preserved, and that it has the only and final authority essentially and effectively on all matters of faith and practice in English-speaking countries.[141,142] In addition, Ruckmanism forces other countries to use only the King James Version. Taking one step further, Ruckmanism never recognizes the limitations of the King James Version as 'translation': trying to put 'translation' in the place of 'text,' or even more, 'translation' over 'text.' Ruckmanism places too much confidence in the accuracy and faithfulness of the translation of the King James Version, leading to the misrepresentation that the King James Version not only surpasses the original texts, but also provides advanced revelations. So, such an idea of Ruckmanism even claims the inspiration of the King James Version like its original texts and the uselessness of the original languages in understanding the Bible. Moreover, Ruckmanism not only has no hesitation to say that the King James Version is inerrant and infallible, but even asserts that it is "the last and final statement" which God has given to the world.[143] The above view of Ruckmanism brought about serious doctrinal and practical problems. As a result, Ruckmanism decries those who disagree with its idea or use the modern versions as 'cults.' However, Ruckmanism exhibits a rather cultic tendency, claiming the speculations that are not based on the Bible at all (for example, distorted

---

[139] Jeffrey Khoo, *KJV Questions & Answers*, ibid.

[140] Edward F. Hills, *The King James Version Defended*, 217.

[141] Peter S. Ruckman, "The Super Superiority of the King James Bible," *Bible Believers' Bulletin*, vol.32 no.2 (Pensacola, Florida: Bible Baptist Church, February 2008), 1, 5, 7, 9. Ruckman says that the King James Version is not only superior to "any version and any translation in any language," but even to the "originals." He even argues that the "originals" could be corrected based on the King James Version, showing that he is completely confused between 'text' and 'translation.' Furthermore, Ruckman's logic rather criticizes the "originals" based on his arguments in support of the King James Version, not even properly understanding the fundamental features of the "originals" written in Hebrew and Greek by Divine inspiration. In fact, Ruckman's logic and arguments are not different from the modern critics.

[142] James D. Price, *King James Onlyism: A New Sect* (Chattanooga, Tennessee: James D. Price Publisher, 2006), 1.

[143] David W. Cloud, *The Bible Version Question-Answer Database*, 149-151.

views of salvation or angels or matters of marriage) as to be truthful teachings.[144,145,146] All these problems of Ruckmanism are the result of truly serious misunderstanding and even arbitrary misuse of the doctrine of the written Word God gives:

First, the target of Divine inspiration described in 2 Timothy 3:16 is the original Hebrew (Aramaic in part) and Greek texts. However, Ruckmanism claims that the King James Version was also inspired as the most accurate translation of the inspired original texts. This is an overinterpretation of the original meaning of 2 Timothy 3:16 that God inspired the Hebrew (Aramaic in part) and Greek words penned by the human writers. The King James Version can never be the directly inspired Word of the Holy Spirit. However, only in a "derived sense," the King James Version can be considered as "inspired" as the 'translation' that delivers the original texts most accurately and faithfully.[147] But this only means that the King James Version has the authority as the Word of God, and it is never to say that the King James Version, the 'translation,' was once again God-breathed (inspired). This is also a problem of Ruckmanism, associated with the inerrancy and infallibility of the King James Version which it claims. Despite the accurate and excellent translation of the King James Version, it cannot guarantee the perfection equivalent to its original texts. Since the King James Version has a limitation as 'translation,' it is essential to return to the inspired and preserved original texts, inerrant and infallible, written in the original languages, to confirm the original meaning and to understand clearly and correctly.[148]

Second, there is no further revelation since the writing of the last verse in the last chapter of the Revelation marked the period and thereby completed the entire 66 books of the Bible: That is, the God-breathed Word written in God-chosen original languages was completely closed with the last verse of the last chapter of Revelation (the Old Testament written in Hebrew from Genesis to Malachi, and the New Testament written in Greek from Matthew to Revelation). This is evident in Revelation 22:18-19 through the serious and strict warning of God, 'the Law of Inalterability,' which never permit any alteration henceforward. The complete Bible (i.e. its original texts) was sealed by God's declarative warning and command. Ruckmanism, however, claims "advanced revelations" through the King James Version, saying that the revelation was ended after the Greek New Testament and then re-ended with the authorized version in 1611.[149] Even saying the King James Version is "the last and final statement that God has given the world,"[150] Ruckmanism claims its final authority. This logic of Ruckmanism runs counter

---

[144] David W. Cloud, *What About Ruckman?* (Oak Harbor, Washington: Way of Life Literature, 1995), 13-15, 21-23.

[145] David W. Cloud, *The Bible Version Question-Answer Database*, 152, 154-156.

[146] Korea also has the "Word of God Preservation Society" that inherits Ruckmanism, and because of this tendency, it has already been defined as a heresy by the major conservative denominations in Korea.

[147] Jeffrey Khoo, *KJV Questions & Answers*, 8.

[148] Ibid.

[149] Peter S. Ruckman, "Advanced Revelations in the King's English," *Bible Believers' Bulletin*, vol.33 no.1 (Pensacola, Florida: Bible Baptist Church, January 2009), 1, 3, 7-8.

[150] Calvin George, "The Danger of Ruckmanism as Applied to Foreign Language Bibles," LITERATURA BAUTISTA, accessed on September 03, 2020, https://en.literaturabautista.com/danger-

to the truth about the inspiration and preservation of God's Word, which is clearly identified even in the King James Version it so advocates. Not only that, Ruckmanism also commits a fatal error of reversing 'translation' with 'text' that was sealed by God upon its completion.

Third, it is true that the King James Version is the Word of God 'in English.' But this is because the King James Version is the most accurate and faithful 'translation of the preserved original texts' into English. In other words, the King James Version is the Word as a 'translation' because of the excellency of its translation that most accurately reflects the inspired and preserved texts. None of the existing translated versions are as faithful and accurate to the original Scriptures as the King James Version does. It is the King James Version that has faithfully served to deliver the inspired and preserved Word of God through the translation of the godly and prominent translators, who were used as the instruments under the guidance of the Holy Spirit: but it is only as a 'translation.' Without acknowledging this obvious fact and its limitation, Ruckmanism is erring beyond the line clearly drawn by God Himself through His Word.

A common problem found in the ideas that Ruckmanism claims is the confusion between 'text' and 'translation.' Of course, Ruckmanism's confidence in Verbal Plenary Inspiration and Preservation and its intent to fulfill human responsibility for those doctrines cannot be blamed as bad. However, in such process, the problem is that Ruckmanism's misunderstanding, misinterpretation and misjudgment of those doctrines are combined with its overconfidence, and eventually its logic flows into a completely wrong direction, not into the truth. As a result, even though it should have stopped at 'translation,' Ruckmanism is committing the error of arbitrarily prioritizing and absolutizing 'translation' over 'text' that God had uttered and wrote. This is the same as Ruckmanism's overlooking and going beyond the deserved scope of the mode and attitude towards the inspired and preserved Word that God says in 'the Law of Inalterability.' Falling short of God's Word is of course a problem, but overshooting the Word is also a problem: Loyalty to the Word must also be done within the scope of what God says in His Word. Excessive loyalty that is not based on a proper understanding of the principles of the Word is likely to lead to false convictions, and the combination of the two (excessive loyalty and false convictions) results in misrepresenting and distorting the truth. Likewise, Ruckmanism commits the error of placing the God-inspired written original texts underneath or at a lower level than their translation, because of its excessive loyalty and false convictions. By clinging to the wrong object, Ruckmanism creates a rather heretical and fanatical phenomenon that serves those unbiblical and erroneous ideas. Although Ruckmanism began with the intention of defending the Word, this phenomenon ironically stems from the overconfidence of Ruckman's own ideas based on his ignorance of the Word. 'The Law of Inalterability,' which God has commanded for the proper mode and attitude of man in dealing with His Word, is a grave human

---

ruckmanism. Calvin George cites this from Peter Ruckman's book, *The Monarch of the Books* (Pensacola, 1973).

responsibility to bear in mind as one who knows the truth of Verbal Plenary Inspiration and Preservation. Hence, one must be loyal to this law of God and the commands contained therein in a manner of humility and obedience. That is what is deserved as the "stewards of the mysteries of God" (1 Cor 4:1-2). But that loyalty, too, must be properly understood and practiced within the scope of God's Word: neither short nor beyond. Westminster Shorter Catechism Question No.14 defines 'sin' as: "Sin is any want of conformity unto, or transgression of, the law of God."[151] In other words, rejecting or denying the truth of God because of not reaching 'the Law of Inalterability' is a serious sin before God; but going beyond the line clearly drawn by God ("not to think of himself more highly than he ought to think," Rom 12:3) with claiming what is not in the Bible as if it were therein is also an equally serious sin as much as in the previous case. Ruckmanism ostensibly claims to be 'for the Word,' but in reality, it is like putting man's thoughts and judgments in the place of God's Word. It is not loyalty to the Word, but pride against the Word: putting human ideas in the place of truth. In fact, the error of Ruckmanism is in line with that of the modern critics: putting man's reason, thoughts, and judgment above God's Word. Ruckmanism and the modern critics are just claiming the same error at both opposite ends of extremes.

---

[151] "Westminster Shorter Catechism - Q14," Bible Presbyterian Church General Synod, accessed July 12, 2020, https://bpc.org/?page_id=341.

CHAPTER III. EMPIRICAL STUDY: VIOLATION OF THE LAW OF INALTERABILITY

3.1 Verbal Plenary Preservation, the Law of Inalterability, and Text

Despite God's clear promises in His Word, unbelief in Verbal Plenary Preservation sparked the modern critics' obsession with amending the original texts. As the instrument for the preservation of God's Word, the traditional and received Greek text that has been verified and transmitted through the faithful and true Church of Jesus Christ have certainly existed: That is the *Textus Receptus*. The Hebrew text has been thoroughly preserved in Israel's traditions and history, so there have been relatively few fights against arbitrary and intentional alteration or error. By comparison, the Greek texts have suffered from a qualitative decline due to intentional alterations or errors since the completion of the New Testament. Thus, while discerning the autographs that God wrote and their apographs He has preserved from these attacks, constant verification has been carried out to apply and transmit the *Textus Receptus* properly. Of course, after the completion of printing the *Textus Receptus*, it was fixed and has been no change therein excluding a bit minor differences like spelling or accents.[152] All those pains were Satan's ingenious strategies and aggressive attacks to make people deny the authenticity and orthodoxy of the perfect Bible; and the attacks continue to this day.

Even in the battle against those constant attacks on the perfect Bible, the perfect Bible has been passed down uninterruptedly through discernment and verification by the faithful and true churches since the Apostolic period. This is because Verbal Plenary Preservation, the promise of God the original Author, has been thoroughly and perfectly kept. However, the corrupted manuscripts, which were discarded by the early churches due to their errors and low quality, rather have been promoted in modern times. In doing so, they came to the forefront of the modern critics as the source of their textual criticism, the representative of which was Westcott and Hort text (1881) edited by Westcott and Hort; And the most representative Greek text published based on the critical text of Westcott and Hort is the Nestle-Aland Greek text (*Novum Testamentum Graece*).

Brief History of the Nestle-Aland Editions[153]: Constant Change and Instability

The *Novum Testamentum Graece*, now called "Nestle-Aland," began its long history of the editions with the first edition published in 1898 by Eberhard Nestle for the purpose of spreading textual criticism. The *Novum Testamentum Graece* was initially based on Tischendorf, Westcott and Hort, and Weymouth, which were known as the leading Greek New Testament scholars in academic circles at that time (later, Weymouth

---

[152] "The History of the *Textus Receptus*," *Textus Receptus* Bibles, accessed on October 10, 2021, http://textusreceptusbibles.com/History.

[153] "History of the Nestle-Aland Edition," Nestle-Aland *Novum Testamentum Graece*, accessed on July 14, 2020, https://www.nestle-aland.com/en/history.

was replaced by Bernhard Weiß). At the beginning of it, there were two major apparatuses commonly used in the compilation of the *Novum Testamentum Graece*, and the first and most basic was textual criticism. Its second apparatus was the continued use of separate critical apparatus such as several manuscripts, early translations, and patristic citations, which were additionally introduced to the Codex Bezae by Erwin Nestle (son of Eberhard Nestle) when the 13th edition was published in 1927. However, they were from editions that were not the primary sources; And from this point onward,[154] it "began to abandon the major reading principle."[155] However, this trend began to change when Kurt Aland joined the editorial in the mid-20th century and applied a radically new approach. In particular, in the 26th edition that was published in 1979, it changed from a method of selecting only the text supported by a majority of the critical editions until that time, to a method based on the source materials, such as newly discovered early papyri and other manuscripts. Thus, the 26th edition was identical to the 3rd edition of the United Bible Societies (UBS, hereafter) Greek New Testament, which was published in 1975. This is because Kurt Aland, who had been already included in the editorial committee of the UBS Greek New Testament since 1955 and also involved in the editorial work of Nestle-Aland simultaneously, contributed to the identicality of both editions in establishing the text. Nevertheless, the appearances or structures of both sides were still different, because the purpose of the compilation of both editions was different: the UBS Greek New Testament is for translation, aiming to provide an apparatus for textual critique, which can show a Greek initial text and various readings required for translation; On the other hand, the Nestle-Aland Greek New Testament is for research, aiming for the critical assessment necessary to reconstruct the Greek initial text for academic education and pastoral practice. And since the 27th edition was revised on the extension of the 26th edition, the text itself did not change. As mentioned above, Kurt Aland and Barbara Aland, who contributed much to the compilation of the Nestle-Aland Greek text, have presented twelve basic rules for New Testament textual criticism:[156]

1. Only one reading can be original, however many variant readings there maybe. Only in very rare instances does the tenacity of the New Testament tradition present an insoluble tie between two or more alternative readings. Textual difficulties should not be solved by conjecture, or by positing glosses or interpolations, etc., where the textual tradition itself shows no break; such attempts amount to capitulation before the difficulties and are themselves violations of the text.
2. Only the readings which best satisfies the requirements of both external and internal criteria can be original.
3. Criticism of the text must always begin from the evidence of the manuscript tradition and only afterward turn to a consideration of internal criteria.

---

[154] Edward D. Andrews, *THE KING JAMES BIBLE: Why Have Modern Why Have Modern Bible Translations Removed Many Verses That Are In the King James Version?* (Cambridge, Ohio: Christian Publishing House, 2019), pp.128-129.

[155] "Nestle Aland," Theopedia, accessed on October 10, 2021, https://www.theopedia.com/nestle-aland.

[156] Kurt Aland and Barbara Aland, *The Text of the New Testament: As Introduction to the Critical Editions and to the Theory and Practice of Textual Criticism*, ibid.

4. Internal criteria (the context of the passage, its style and vocabulary, the theological environment of the author, etc.) can never be the sole basis for a critical decision, especially in opposition to the external evidence.

5. The primary authority for a critical textual decision lies with the Greek manuscript tradition, with the versions and Fathers serving no more than a supplementary and corroborative function, particularly in passages where their underlying Greek text cannot be reconstructed with absolute certainty.

6. Furthermore, manuscripts should be weighed, not counted, and the peculiar traits of each manuscript should be duly considered. However important the early papyri, or a particular uncial, or a minuscule may be, there is no single manuscript or group of manuscripts that can be followed mechanically, even though certain combinations of witnesses may deserve a greater degree of confidence than others. Rather, decisions in textual criticism must be worked out afresh, passage by passage (the local principle).

7. The principle that the original reading may be found in any single manuscript or version when it stands alone or nearly alone is only a theoretical possibility. Any form of eclecticism which accepts this principle will hardly succeed in establishing the original text of the New Testament; it will only confirm the view of the text which it presupposes.

8. The reconstruction of a stemma of readings for each variant (the genealogical principle) is an extremely important device, because the reading which can most easily explain the derivation of the other forms is itself most likely the original.

9. Variants must never be treated in isolation, but always considered in the context of the tradition. Otherwise there is too great a danger of reconstructing a "test tube text" which never existed at any time or place.

10. There is truth in the maxim: *lectio difficilior lectio potior* ("the more difficult reading is the more probable reading"). But this principle must not be taken too mechanically, with the most difficult reading (*lectio difficilima*) adopted as original simply because of its degree of difficulty.

11. The venerable maxim *lectio brevior lectio potior* ("the shorter reading is the more probable reading") is certainly right in many instances. But here again the principle cannot be applied mechanically. It is not valid for witnesses whose texts otherwise vary significantly from the characteristic patterns of the textual tradition, with frequent omissions or expansions reflecting editorial tendencies (e.g., D). Neither should the commonly accepted rule of thumb that variants agreeing with parallel passages or with the Septuagint in Old Testament quotations are secondary be applied in a purely mechanical way. A blind consistency can be just as dangerous here as in Rule 10 (*lectio difficilior*).

12. A constantly maintained familiarity with New Testament manuscripts themselves is the best training for textual criticism. Anyone interested in contributing seriously to textual criticism should have the experience of making a complete collation of at least one of the great early papyri, a major uncial, and one of the significant minuscule manuscripts. In textual criticism the pure theoretician has often done more harm than good.

Their basic rules show how the Nestle-Aland Greek text, as the representative of the Greek critical texts, has been edited, and basically the logic of textual criticism is deeply embedded in it. Their logic and methodology are basically based on the unbelief in Verbal Plenary Preservation. So, the modern critics never stop trying to establish the text closest to the originals by reconstructing it from variant readings. The problem is that too many human thoughts and judgments are arbitrarily involved in their criteria for determining its authenticity. For this reason, their standards cannot be God-oriented and thus utterly distant from the Bible, the principles of which God Himself gave in the Word. God already wrote and has been preserved His own principles in His Word, and all we have to do is just wholly obey 'the' principles of the Word: not human criteria.

3.2 Empirical Methodology
3.2.1 *Textus Receptus* versus Nestle-Aland 27th/28th Editions[157]

The most recent version of the Nestle-Aland Greek text is the 28th edition published in 2012, a revision of 20 years since 1993 when the first round of its 27th edition was published. As noted earlier, the 27th edition is the extensive revision of the 26th edition identical to the 3rd edition of the UBS Greek New Testament, and they all remained highly dependent on newly discovered manuscripts. However, the 28th edition of the Nestle-Aland Greek text underwent 'a major change in its methodology once again.' The main difference between two editions (the 27th and the 28th) is that 'a new critical methodology' was engaged. After the 27th edition, the *Editio Critica Maior* (ECM; a critical edition) of the Greek New Testament, based on all possible manuscripts and other sources, was released; and both texts (the UBS Greek New Testament and the Nestle-Aland Greek text) adopted it for their editing. According to the new editing standards they had applied up to that time, the *Editio Critica Maior* of the Greek New Testament was obviously a newly available material. Thus, the 28th edition of the Nestle-Aland Text was edited based on the *Editio Critica Maior* of the Greek New Testament, with the goal of achieving two different tasks: First, thoroughly editing the apparatus to make it clearer and easier to be used; Second, getting insights and making decisions about textual critique based on this new source material (the *Editio Critica Maior* of the Greek New Testament). On the basis of this new methodology, it is the Nestle-Aland 28th edition that had undergone thorough inspection and rearrangement of the apparatus without changing the basic structure. This methodological change also applied to the UBS Greek New Testament 5th edition, which shared the same source material as the Nestle-Aland Greek text.

3.2.2 General Epistles

The transition of the methodology that led to a sweeping change from the Nestle-Aland 27th edition to the 28th edition was applied first to only the General Epistles, not to the entire New Testament, as of 2012. This is because there had been a significant change in the textual-critical apparatus of the General Epistles in the *Editio Critica Maior*, which was the basis of the Nestle-Aland 28th edition and the UBS Greek New Testament 5th edition. The *Editio Critica Maior* used G. Mink's Coherence-Based Genealogical

---

[157] Barbara Aland, Kurt Aland, Johannes Karavidopoulos, Carlo M. Martini, and Bruce M. Metzger, eds., *Nestle-Aland Novum Testamentum Graece: Based on the work of Eberhard and Erwin Nestle*, 28th rev. ed. (Stuttgart, Germany: Deutsche Bibelgesellschaft, 2012), 46-48.

Method, a hybrid method which was developed using both computer analysis based on evolutionary biology and traditional text-critical methods. And this method was also applied to the General Epistles of the Nestle-Aland *Novum Testamentum Graece*.[158,159,160] Thus, there were also other minor structural edits, but the section of the New Testament that showed the most striking difference between the 27th and 28th editions was the General Epistles (James, 1 Peter, 2 Peter, 1 John, 2 John, 3 John, and Jude).

Meanwhile, papers addressing the changes between the 27th and 28th editions are rare, and it is also the case that no study thus far has conducted a comparative analysis between the Nestle-Aland 28th edition and the *Textus Receptus*. In 2006, J. A. Moorman examined the differences between the Nestle-Aland 26th/27th edition and the *Textus Receptus*, revealing that there were over 8,000 differences between the two Greek texts.[161] Jang Dong Soo studied the UBS Greek New Testament 5th edition, which was published in 2014 following the Nestle-Aland 28th edition published in 2012. As mentioned in the introductory section to the Nestle-Aland 28th edition, it and the UBS Greek New Testament 5th edition are substantially identical because they used the same source material. Therefore, although the publishing purposes of the two texts were different from each other, the methodology and consequential characteristics used in the UBS Greek New Testament 5th edition were the same as the Nestle-Aland 28th edition. In his research, Jang Dong Soo pointed out that, compared to the 4th edition, new critical apparatuses were added to the text of the UBS Greek New Testament 5th edition and overall revisions such as paragraph breaks were made. However, in the UBS Greek New Testament 5th edition, the most epoch-making and significant changes appeared in the General Epistles, highlighting that the methodological change already mentioned above made a significant difference, especially in text-related decisions.[162]

---

[158] Dong Soo Jang, "A Study on the Text Changes in the United Bible Society Greek New Testament 5th Edition," *Journal of the Biblical Text Research*, vol.39 (Seoul, Korea: The Institute for Biblical Text Research of the Korean Bible Society, October 2016), 266-287. The Coherence-Based Genealogical Method first identifies the ancestor-descendant relationship of multiple variant readings, to find its local *stemma* for each variant, and then creates the most optimal *substemma*. After that, the initial text is constructed by creating the global *stemma* based on the most optimal *substemm*. Through all these processes, it is the aim of the Coherence-Based Genealogical Method to grasp the history that the text has been transmitted through the copy.

[159] Yii-Jan Lin, *The Erotic Life of Manuscripts: New Testament Textual Criticism and the Biological Sciences* (New York, NY: Oxford University Press, 2016), 124-125.

[160] Tommy Wasserman and Peter J. Gurry, *A New Approach to Textual Criticism: An Introduction to the Coherence-Based Genealogical Method* (Atlanta, GA: Society of Biblical Literature, 2017; Stuttgart, Germany: Deutsche Bibelgesellschaft, 2017), 21-26. The problem is that this method in which they engage as 'new' presupposes the contamination of the New Testament manuscripts and the intervention of coincidences. Not only does this signify the fatal limitations inherent in it, but the premise itself clearly reveals that the Divine preservation of the perfect Bible by the original Author Himself is not at all under their consideration.

[161] Jack Moorman, *8,000 Differences Between the N.T. Greek Words of the King James Bible and the Modern Versions*, ibid.

[162] Dong Soo Jang, ibid.

3.2.3 Empirical Methodology for Comparative Analysis

As discussed above, there have been some papers that have studied the differences between the Nestle-Aland 26th/27th edition and the *Textus Receptus*, or the changes in the UBS Greek New Testament 5th edition identical to the Nestle-Aland 28th edition. However, no paper has considered together the differences between the Nestle-Aland 28th edition and the *Textus Receptus* and how the Nestle-Aland 28th edition differs from the aspects seen in the previous stage, the Nestle-Aland 27th edition. Therefore, in this study, the Nestle-Aland 28th edition is compared with the *Textus Receptus* in order to observe the recent trend happening in the critical Greek text, in light of Verbal Plenary Preservation and the Law of Inalterability. In addition, the difference between the Nestle-Aland 28th edition and the *Textus Receptus* is observed compared to the difference between its previous (27th) edition and the *Textus Receptus* founded by J. A. Moorman. Based on the traditional received text (the *Textus Receptus*) that God has preserved as promised, by observing the trend of the differences in both editions (the 27th and the 28th) of the Nestle-Aland Greek text, it is possible to see for which direction the Nestle-Aland 28th edition is heading. And, as well as whether there are differences between those three texts mentioned above (the Nestle-Aland 27th/28th edition and the *Textus Receptus*), the types of differences (change, addition or deletion) are classified together. Through all of these classifications, this study will determine whether the Nestle-Aland 28th edition is getting closer to the *Textus Receptus* (positive/good, 'Toward'), or rather getting farther away from it (negative/bad, 'Away From').

And since the new methodology was effectively applied only to the General Epistles in the Nestle-Aland 28th edition, its previous study was also conducted for the General Epistles. Therefore, this study also targets the General Epistles, conducting analyses not only of the 'longitudinal' changes ('NA27' vs. 'NA28') of the Nestle-Aland Greek texts, but also of the 'cross-sectional' changes comparing each of the two editions with the *Textus Receptus* (i.e. Analyses for 'NA27' vs. 'TR'; and 'NA28' vs. 'TR')

To do so, it is imperative to analyze the basic characteristics of data. In order to promote this, it is necessary to convert qualitative data, 'text difference,' into quantitative data. Therefore, after the difference existence and nonexistence of the target texts (the Nestle-Aland 27th and 28th editions, the *Textus Receptus*), as a whole and by category, are coded as '1 or 0,' this quantified data is used for the empirical analysis. At this time, the basic unit of classification and coding is each verse. And for basic statistical analysis, SAS University Edition is used.

3.3 Empirical Results

3.3.1 Observations: *Textus Receptus* versus Nestle-Aland 27th/28th Editions

The first part examined was the difference between the 27th (NA27) and 28th (NA28) editions of the Nestle-Aland Greek text (Chart 1). A total of 53 cases of 'longitudinal changes' are observed in the General Epistles, where the most changes have been made by the new methodology called the Coherence-Based Genealogical Method. In other words, as the Nestle-Aland Greek text was revised to the 28th edition (NA28), 53 verses of the General Epistles were different in the 28th edition (NA28) compared to the 27th edition (NA27). The book with the most cumulative differences among the General Epistles is 1 Peter, followed by 2 Peter, James, and 1 John. A total of 18 verses from 1 Peter, 12 verses from 2 Peter, and 9 verses each from James and 1 John were revised in the 28th edition (NA28). However, considering the number of chapters included in each book, the averaged frequency of the differences per chapter is also presented in parentheses. However, the average verse frequency of the differences per chapter is also most frequently observed in 2 Peter (4 verses revised per chapter) and 1 Peter (3.6 verses revised per chapter).

Chart 1: Difference (NA27, NA28)
- Verse Frequency (Average Verse Frequency Per Chapter) -

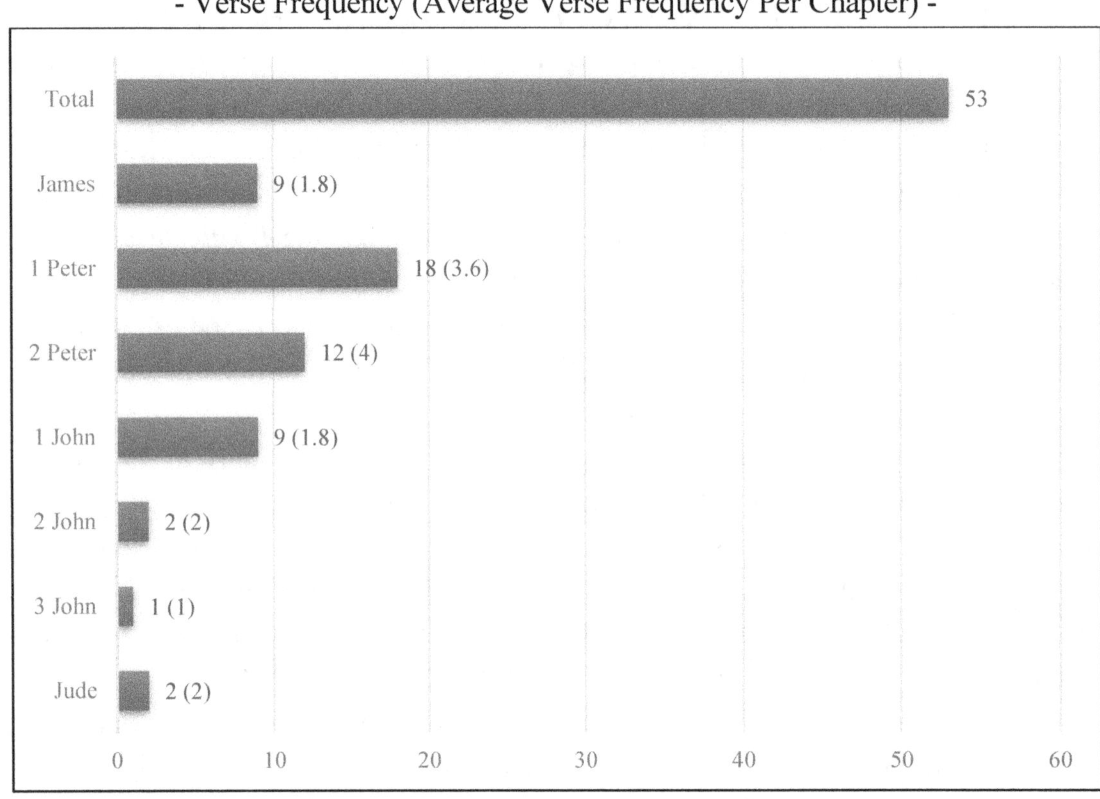

Next is the result of the analysis of the 'cross-sectional changes,' comparing each edition of the Nestle-Aland Greek text with the *Textus Receptus* (Chart 2). The Nestle-Aland 27th edition (NA27) differs from the *Textus Receptus* in the General Epistle by 230 verses, while its 28th edition (NA28) does by 213 verses: The difference from the *Textus Receptus* decreased by 17 verses.[163] The book with the greatest cumulative difference from the *Textus Receptus* is 1 Peter in both the 27th and 28th editions: the 27th edition (NA27) differs from the *Textus Receptus* in 62 verses of 1 Peter, but the 28th edition (NA28) shows that the difference has decreased to 56 verses in 1 Peter. Following 1 Peter,

---

[163] These differences (total and by each book) are the cumulative values of the verses, coded as 1 if a verse contains more than one kind of alteration: That is, the coding value is 1 regardless of whether any verse has one alteration or more. Thus, this frequency means the cumulative sum of those coding values.

James and 1 John of the Nestle-Aland 27th and 28th editions show high cumulative differences from the *Textus Receptus*.

Chart 2: Difference (NA27, TR) vs. Difference (NA28, TR)
- Verse Frequency (Average Verse Frequency Per Chapter) -

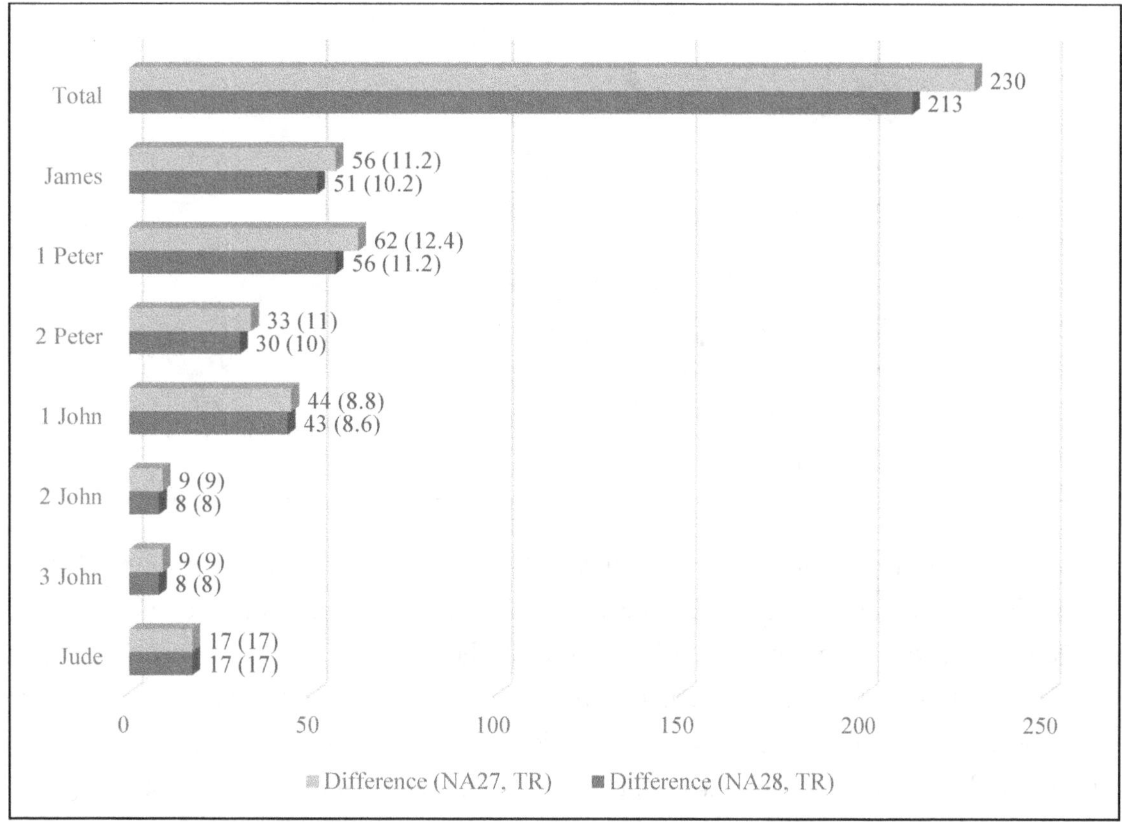

However, when considering the number of chapters contained in each book, the book with the greatest mean difference from the *Textus Receptus* per chapter is rather Jude: despite having only one chapter, both Nestle-Aland editions show the same difference of 17 verses compared to the *Textus Receptus* in Jude. Jude has a total of 25 verses, which means that most of them (68%) differ from the *Textus Receptus* even in this one chapter. Most of the causes of such a great difference in Jude are that the Nestle-Aland 27th (NA27) and 28th (NA28) editions have deleted certain words from the *Textus Receptus* (the 27th - 7 verses, the 28th - 6 verses) or changed to other words (the 27th and 28th, both are 6 verses). For example, in Jude 5, ὁ Κύριος in the *Textus Receptus* was replaced by Ἰησοῦς in the Nestle-Aland 28th edition with deletion of the definite article. In Jude 18, the Nestle-Aland 28th edition also deleted the conjunction ὅτι from ὅτι ἐν ἐσχάτῳ χρόνῳ of the *Textus Receptus*. Along with that, the preposition ἐν was also changed to ἐπ᾽, and this change even turned dative cases (ἐσχάτῳ χρόνῳ) completely into genitive cases (ἐσχάτου χρόνου).

Chart 3: Alterations (NA27, TR) vs. Alterations (NA28, TR)
- Case Frequency (Verse Frequency) -

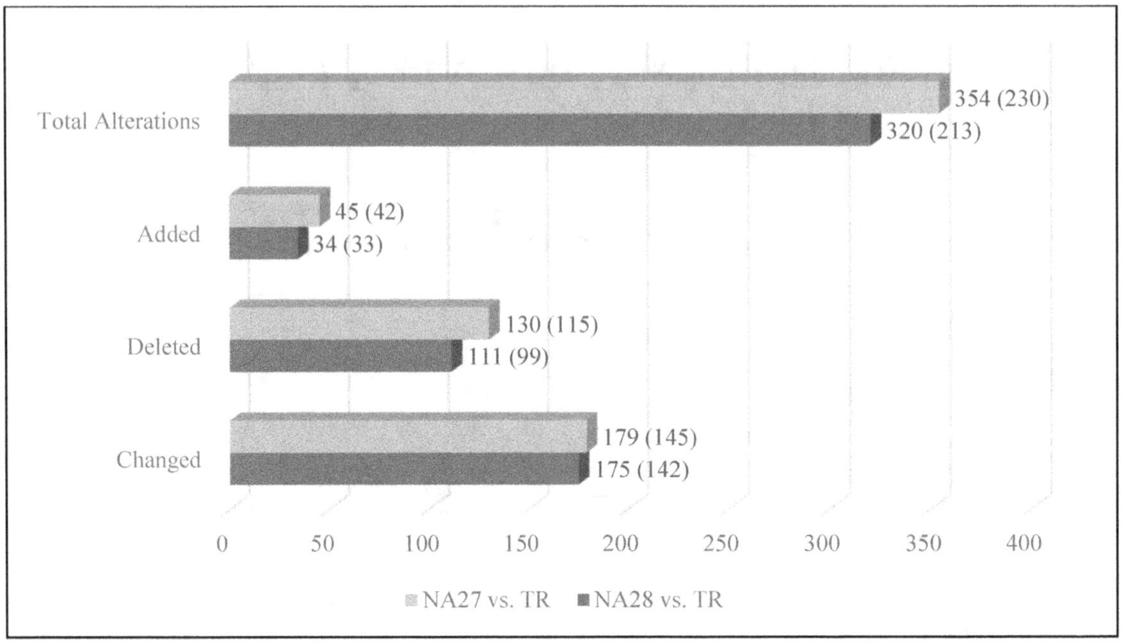

The third diagram (Chart 3) shows the frequency of total alterations that is accumulated all observed differences by type, after classifying what type (Added/Deleted/Changed) of each difference from the *Textus Receptus* is observed in the General Epistles of two Nestle-Aland editions (NA27/NA28). From this, it is possible to understand what kinds of alterations were made compared to the *Textus Receptus* in both editions of the Nestle Aland Greek text, and how the patterns of those alterations changed with the revision to the 28th edition. First, differences from the *Textus Receptus* were observed in a total of 354 cases from the Nestle-Aland 27th edition and 320 cases from its 28th edition. Although 230 verses (NA27) and 213 verses (NA28) were respectively reported in Chart 2, for the differences from the *Textus Receptus* in both editions, more cases were presented in Chart 3. The reason is that there were many verses in which multiple causes of difference (i.e., multiple cases) were identified within each verse. The Nestle-Aland 27th edition reports 45 cases of 'Added' from 42 verses and 130 cases of 'Deleted' from 115 verses out of a total of 354 cases. In addition, 179 cases were found from 145 verses of 'Changed' that changes the words recorded in the *Textus Receptus* to another words. This is just over half of the total alterations in the 27th edition (50.6%). On the other hand, in the Nestle-Aland 28th edition, 34 cases of 'Added' from 33 verses and 111 cases of 'Deleted' from 99 verses were observed among a total of 320 cases. 'Changed' also held the highest share of total alterations in the 28th edition. Its total frequency is 175 cases from 142 verses, which is a higher proportion (54.7%) than the 27th edition (50.6%). Anyway, with revision to the 28th edition, the frequencies of all three types decreased.

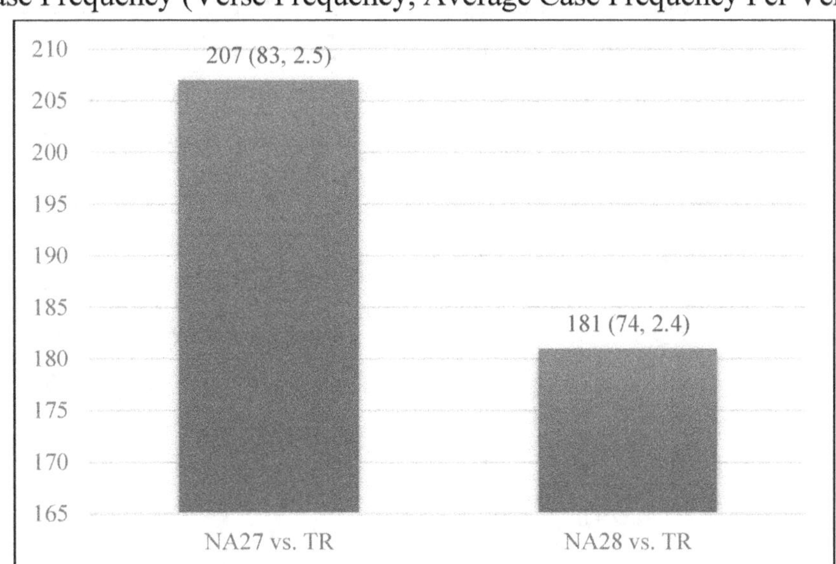

Chart 4 presents the cases where alterations are made for more than one type in one verse, mentioned earlier in Chart 3. In other words, it counts all the cases where the differences of the Nestle-Aland 27th and 28th editions from the *Textus Receptus* appear in more than one type among three types of alterations (Added/Deleted/Changed) within one verse. In the Nestle-Aland 27th edition, a total of 207 cases of these multicausal alterations were extracted from 83 verses, meaning that on average there are 2.5 multiple causes per verse. Meanwhile, in the 28th edition, a total of 181 cases of multicausal alterations were identified from 74 verses. This differs from the *Textus Receptus* due to an average of 2.4 multiple causes per one verse. Nevertheless, as in Chart 3, as revised to the 28th edition, the total frequency of multicausal alterations also declined, including cases as well as verses and their averages. When considering Chart 3 and Chart 4 together, observing these results from a different angle can be interpreted as showing the concentration of multicausal alterations. This is pretty interesting: Besides the verses for which only one causal factor was identified (147 and 139 cases/verses for the 27th and 28th editions, respectively), since only 36%/35% of verses produced 58%/57% of multicausal cases for the 27th/28th editions. Despite a decrease of 1% in the 28th edition, such results, which are almost consistent in both editions, suggest that more varied and intensive alterations were made in fewer verses.

Table 1 is the result of classifying the multicausal alterations presented in Chart 4 by book for each edition. In the Nestle-Aland 27th edition, the book with the highest total case frequency of multicausal alterations was 1 Peter (52 cases from 21 verses), followed by James (50 cases from 19 verses). However, the average frequency obtained by dividing the total cases in which multicausal alterations were observed by the number of corresponding verses was highest in Jude. In Jude, the differences from the *Textus Receptus* occurred due to multiple causes, which are almost 3 cases per one verse (2.9/verse). However, this difference of Jude slightly decreased as it was revised to the

28th edition, and instead, James reports the highest number not only in total cases but also in average cases per verse (total 46 cases; 2.7 cases per verse). Following James, it is 2 Peter that the average frequency of cases per verse is relatively high. In 2 Peter, on average, 2.6 cases of the multiple causes of difference were observed in one verse. These multicausal alterations can be said to show how various distortions have been attempted in the critical texts compared to the *Textus Receptus*.

Table 1: Cross-Frequency of Multicausal Alteration by Book

	NA27 vs. TR			NA28 vs. TR		
	N (cases)	N (verses)	N (cases/verse)	N (cases)	N (verses)	N (cases/verse)
James	50	19	2.6	46	17	2.7
1 Peter	52	21	2.5	42	17	2.5
2 Peter	44	18	2.4	36	14	2.6
1 John	26	11	2.4	26	12	2.2
2 John	7	3	2.3	6	3	2.0
3 John	8	4	2.0	8	4	2.0
Jude	20	7	2.9	17	7	2.4
Total	207 (of 354)	83	2.5	181 (of 320)	74	2.4

In relation to the three types of alterations (Changed/Added/Deleted) examined in Chart 3, the total cumulative frequency of the subtypes for each of the three types is presented in Table 2. First, the subtypes of 'Changed' include 'Word, Letter, Order, Case, Tense, Number, Gender' (Section A of Table 2). Among them, the most frequently observed in both editions is the change in 'Word.' This means that the cases where the Nestle-Aland Greek text has changed the words from the *Textus Receptus* are 71 and 68 in the 27th and 28th editions, respectively. The books with the most 'Word' observed in both editions are all 1 Peter, followed by James. In the Nestle-Aland Greek text, the next most 'Changed' type after 'Word' was 'Letter,' and 36 cases were found in both the 27th and 28th editions. The third ranking is 'Order,' slightly reduced from 30 cases in the 27th edition to 28 cases in the 28th edition. The most distinctive feature of the 'Changed' type is 'Gender,' which is the arbitrary change of the gender of the participle in 1 Peter 2:25. The first sentence of 1 Peter 2:25 is ἦτε γὰρ ὡς πρόβατα πλανώμενα in the *Textus Receptus*. However, all of the Nestle-Aland Greek texts (both the 27th and 28th editions) regard participle πλανώμενα, which modifies πρόβατα, as for ἦτε, and change the neuter plural participle (πλανώμενα) to the masculine plural participle (πλανώμενοι). This is not only a change of 'Gender,' but also reflects the editors' arbitrary interpretation of the sentence structure.

Meanwhile, the case of adding something to the *Textus Receptus* decreased from 45 cases in the 27th edition to 34 cases in the 28th edition. (Section B of Table 2). Among the subtypes under 'Added,' the most frequent case is the addition of 'Word,' which is nearly 50% in the 28th edition. The addition of 'Conjunction' is closely following 'Word.'

Other than that, the unique phenomenon in 'Added' is 'Negative.' This is observed from 2 Peter 3:10 only in the 28th edition, adding the negative marker (οὐχ), which is not originally present in the *Textus Receptus*. However, this is not just a matter of οὐχ, but the result of changing the verb κατακαήσεται (shall be burned up) recorded in the *Textus Receptus* to οὐχ εὑρεθήσεται (not will be found). This is not simply a matter of the Nestle-Aland Greek text, but of the Westcott and Hort Greek New Testament upon which it is based; and even before them, of the *Textus Criticus*, the cause of all critical texts. In other words, this sudden and 180-degree change is a problem that has been chained since the family of the *Textus Criticus* such as ℵ (Codex Sinaiticus), *B* (Codex Vaticanus) arbitrarily altered κατακαήσεται selected and written by its original Author (i.e. God Himself) into εὑρεθήσεται for paraphrase in the earlier centuries.[164,165,166] Thus, in the Nestle-Aland 28th edition, this negative marker (οὐχ), which was not there before, seems to be included into the text as a kind of attempt to approach εὑρεθήσεται closer to κατακαήσεται in its meaning.

Table 2: Cross-Frequency of Alteration (Changed/Added/Deleted)
by Subtype and Book

Section A. Changed

		Word	Letter	Order	Case	Tense	Number	Gender	Total
NA27 vs. TR	James	15	16	8	1	5	1	0	46
	1 Peter	20	11	2	0	6	2	1	42
	2 Peter	13	4	7	4	2	3	0	33
	1 John	11	1	4	3	7	1	0	27
	2 John	4	1	4	0	1	0	0	10
	3 John	2	1	1	1	1	1	0	7
	Jude	6	2	4	2	0	0	0	14
	Total	71	36	30	11	22	8	1	179
NA28 vs. TR	James	14	16	9	1	5	1	0	46
	1 Peter	18	11	2	1	6	2	1	41
	2 Peter	12	4	7	4	2	3	0	32
	1 John	12	1	4	3	7	1	0	28
	2 John	4	1	2	0	1	0	0	8
	3 John	2	1	1	1	1	1	0	7
	Jude	6	2	3	2	0	0	0	13
	Total	68	36	28	12	22	8	1	175

---

[164] Jay P. Green, Unholy Hands on the Bible, Volume II: An Examination of the Six Major New Versions (Lafayette, Indiana: Sovereign Grace Trust Fund, 1992), 114.

[165] SEE THE MANUSCRIPT, "2 Peter 3:10," Codex Sinaiticus, accessed on November 27, 2021, http://www.codex-sinaiticus.net/en/manuscript.aspx?book=54&chapter=3&lid=en&side=r&verse=10&zoomSlider=0.

[166] Therefore, it is also found that the translated versions based on these corresponding Greek texts follow their paraphrased original Greek term.

Section B. Added

		Conjunction	Article	Negative	Letter	Word	Total
NA27 Vs. TR	James	4	0		1	5	10
	1 Peter	2	2		2	3	9
	2 Peter	2	1		4	3	10
	1 John	5	1	(N/A)	1	2	9
	2 John	0	0		0	0	0
	3 John	0	1		0	2	3
	Jude	0	2		0	2	4
	Total	13	7	(N/A)	8	17	45
NA28 vs. TR	James	4	0	0	0	5	9
	1 Peter	2	0	0	0	3	5
	2 Peter	2	1	1	1	2	7
	1 John	5	1	0	0	2	8
	2 John	0	0	0	0	0	0
	3 John	0	0	0	0	2	2
	Jude	0	1	0	0	2	3
	Total	13	3	1	1	16	34

Section C. Deleted

		Conjunction	Verb	Article	Letter	Word	Total
NA27 vs. TR	James	8	1	6	1	15	31
	1 Peter	6	1	10	4	21	42
	2 Peter	2	0	5	1	8	16
	1 John	3	0	3	0	17	23
	2 John	0	0	0	0	3	3
	3 John	1	0	0	0	2	3
	Jude	2	0	3	0	7	12
	Total	22	2	27	6	73	130
NA28 vs. TR	James	7	0	4	0	14	25
	1 Peter	6	1	6	5	17	35
	2 Peter	2	0	4	1	6	13
	1 John	3	0	3	0	15	21
	2 John	0	0	0	0	3	3
	3 John	1	0	0	0	2	3
	Jude	2	0	3	0	6	11
	Total	21	1	20	6	63	111

In addition to this, it has been found that the editors have arbitrarily deleted what is in the preserved original text, and the tendency has decreased somewhat as it is revised to the 28th edition. Section C of Table 2 reports that 'Deleted' from 130 cases in the 27th edition to 111 cases in the 28th edition: a total of 19 cases decreased. Like other types of alterations, the most frequent 'Deleted' is also of 'Word.' The editors' arbitrary deletion of words is close to 56% and 57% in the 27th and 28th editions, respectively. It was followed by 'Article' in the 27th edition (27 cases). However, in the 28th edition, 'Article' was 20 cases reduced by 7 cases. Other than that, the subtype that occupies a large part of 'Deleted' is 'Conjunction.'

But the most important thing in this empirical analysis is whether the change from the 27th to the 28th edition of the Nestle-Aland Greek text is a good or bad change according to the absolute standard of the *Textus Receptus*, the God-preserved Greek New Testament. That is, it is more important whether the change is a positive and good change that is coming closer to the *Textus Receptus*, or a negative and bad change that is going farther away from it, rather than whether the changes between the 27th and the 28th themselves are there. Therefore, when all the results observed in the above analyses are put together, the results of examining the direction of the Nestle-Aland 28th edition are presented in Chart 5. Among the changes in between the 27th to the 28th, the verses with the 'positive/good' changes (Toward) that are moving closer to the *Textus Receptus* are 43, whereas those with the 'negative/bad' changes that are going farther away from it (Away From) are 15. The total of both changes are 58 verses.[167]

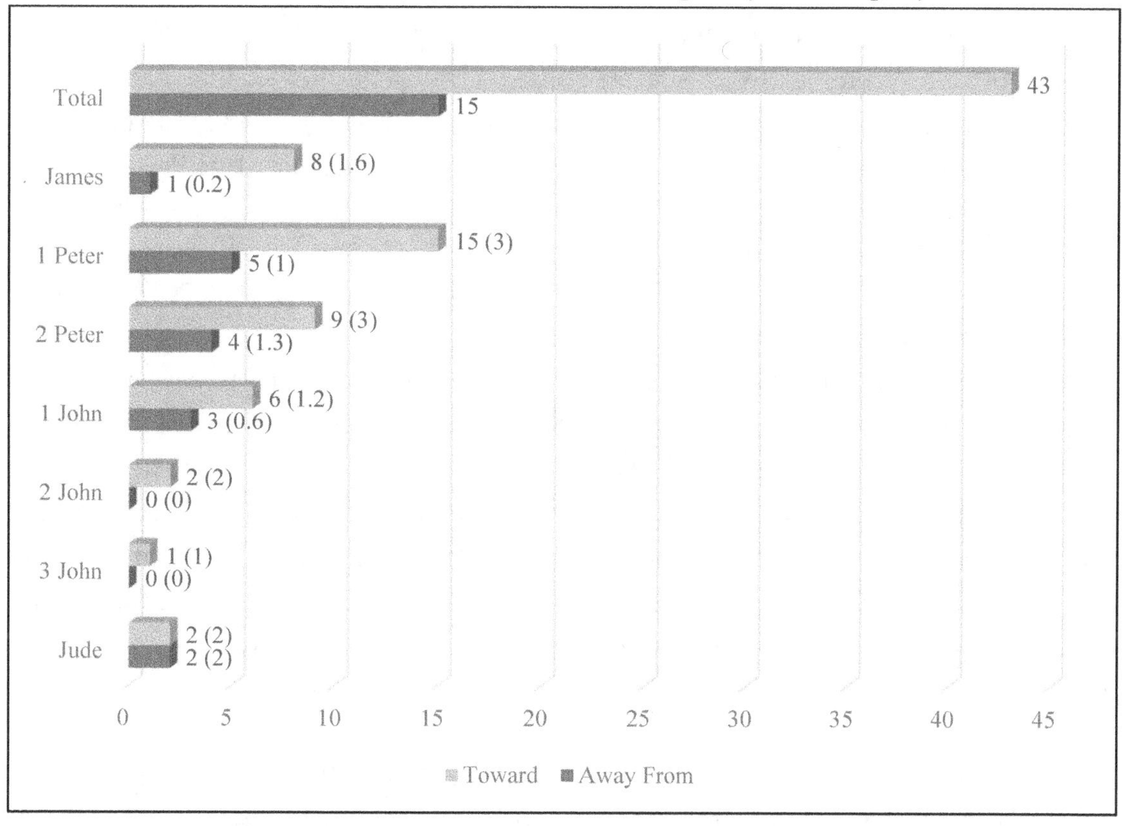

<u>Chart 5: Toward TR vs. Away From TR</u>
- Verse Frequency (Average Verse Frequency Per Chapter) -

---

[167] These 58 verses are higher than the frequency of the longitudinal changes between the 27th and the 28th observed in Chart 1 (53 verses). This is because there are several overlapping cases (5 verses) in which a positive/good change and a negative/bad change are observed simultaneously in one verse: 1 Peter 1:6, 1 Peter 1:16, 2 Peter 3:16, Jude 5, Jude 18.

Such a change from the 27th to the 28th edition of the Nestle-Aland Greek text means that, in the overall trend, its editing was made in a direction closer to the *Textus Receptus*. Among the General Epistles, the books with the highest frequency of the verses with the 'positive/good' changes (Toward) are 1 Peter (15 verses) and 2 Peter (9 verses), each of which has 3 verses also at the highest frequency per chapter. Meanwhile, the books that show the most frequently observed the 'negative/bad' changes (Away From) are 1 Peter - 2 Peter - 1 John - Jude in turn: Jude shows the highest frequency of the verses with the 'negative/bad' changes per chapter. However, except Jude tying in both directions, all the General Epistles have the more 'positive/good' changes than the 'negative/bad' ones. Therefore, it is possible to interpret that the new methodology co-introduced by the Nestle-Aland 28th edition and the UBS Greek text 5th edition (a.k.a. the Coherence-Based Genealogical Method) influenced on their editing in a positive and good way for now.

Finally, a comparison table showing the three target texts themselves (the *Textus Receptus*, the 27th and 28th editions of the Nestle-Aland Greek text), the differences among those texts, and the direction of the revisions to the Nestle-Aland 28th edition is presented in APPENDIX, only for the verses included in Chart 5 (on the positive/good or negative/bad changes compared to the *Textus Receptus*). First of all, there are a total of 53 verses (D2728) in which the differences between the Nestle-Aland 27th and 28th have occurred, consistent with the frequency of Chart 1. The positive/good changes (Toward) that are coming closer to the *Textus Receptus* and the negative/bad changes (Away From) that are going farther away from it are 43 and 15 verses, respectively, consistent with Chart 5 (total 58 verses). From this comparison table of APPENDIX, it is possible to catch which part of the Nestle-Aland Greek texts causes the differences, compared to the *Textus Receptus*.

3.3.2 Violation of the Law of Inalterability

Although a simple frequency analysis is conducted only with the General Epistles, the total cumulative frequency of the differences observed between the Nestle-Aland 27th/28th edition and the *Textus Receptus* is still high. However, one positive aspect of the changes found in the Nestle-Aland 28th edition is that the editing direction of this text is a little closer to the side of the *Textus Receptus*, due to the change in its methodology for editing (due to the introduction of the new methodology, that is, the Coherence-Based Genealogical Method). Nevertheless, there are still significant differences between the Nestle-Aland 28th edition and the *Textus Receptus*.

Critique: Repetition of Editing, Unbelief in the Absolute Truth of God

There is one common problem that is found while examining the history of the Nestle-Aland Greek text, which is a representative of the critical texts, and analyzing its current state through the empirical analysis presented above: that is, whenever the methodologies and standards of text editing change, the outputs of editing also continue to change in new ways. Although the Nestle-Aland 28th edition is getting closer to the

Textus Receptus due to the new methodology, if another source material is found in the future or another methodology for editing is applied, the text may be changed again, or worse into the reverse direction again. As one of the examples of the critics' arbitrary measurement of the Greek text that is also found in the Nestle-Aland 28th edition, some portions that were treated with a square bracket ([ ]) in the Nestle-Aland 27th edition were even removed in the Nestle-Aland 28th edition. (Jas 4:12, Jas 5:14, 1 Peter 1:6, 1 Peter 1:9, 1 Peter 1:12, 1 Peter 1:22, 1 Peter 3:1, 1 Peter 3:22, 1 Peter 4:17, 1 Peter 5:2, 1 Peter 5:5, 2 Peter 2:6, 2 Peter 3:11, 1 John 2:6, 1 John 3:19, 1 John 3:21, 1 John 5:1, Jude 5). The use of the square bracket ([ ]) means that the editors were unable to determine or refrained from ascertaining whether the wording used for that portion was in the original texts. However, the later removal of the square bracket ([ ]) at the discretion of the editors again implies that they have determined and treated the same wording, which was in the square bracket ([ ]) before, as clear again to them. Such decisions and treatments made by the editors show that the certainty and authenticity of God's Word can be altered by the judgment of the editors, who are merely human beings: This is absolutely and completely subjective. More seriously, even in some cases, the square brackets ([ ]) as well as the wordings contained therein were also deleted together: the arbitrary deletion of the Word in 1 Peter 1:16, 1 Peter 2:5, 1 Peter 5:10, 2 Peter 3:18, Jude 5, Jude 18. This is because they treat the weight of God's Word too lightly and are against 'the Law of Inalterability.' Even the basic analysis of this study shows well how low their view of God's Word is. This is inconsistent with the inalterability of God's Word, which implies the nature of His immutability. 'The Law of Inalterability' is not the writer's own dogmatic theory, but a very serious and unavoidable fatal command that God gave directly to all His people through His own written Word. The moment the writing of the entire 66 books was completed, God's written Word was literally fixed and confirmed. He is God who promised to keep His Word forever without any change. Thus, their repeated editing shows their unbelief in 'that' promise of God, the preservation of God's Word (Verbal Plenary Preservation), and their complete disobedience to God's strict command about man's necessary and proper mode and attitude toward His Word ('the Law of Inalterability'). This is a serious dereliction of their duty, ignoring human responsibility as the humble instruments used for the preservation of God's Word, and nothing more than their pride that puts human judgment in the place of God's judgment.

CONCLUSION

Verbal Plenary Preservation is not just a matter to be treated simply as one of many doctrines. It is the promise of God's eternal Word, which the original Author Himself must have preserved. And in dealing with the preserved Word, man must fully accept and respect it, and show faithfulness in and loyalty to it. This is the right mode and attitude that man should take before God's Word; and it is 'the Law of Inalterability,' which God has commanded to apply to the whole Word, from Genesis to Revelation. This law was also written in God's Word, and is still required of us as God has preserved it to this day. So far, Verbal Plenary Preservation has been emphasized only as God's sure keeping of His promise, but this is the doctrine of the Bible from the side of God. This study tried to take one step further to examine 'the Law of Inalterability,' which demands the responsibility given to man (the proper mode and attitude to be taken in the preservation of the Word) as God's humble instrument for Verbal Plenary Preservation. Of course, even if man totally denies God's Word due to his totally depraved nature, God alone is sure to preserve His Word (Mt 5:18): God is all-powerful and sufficient in Himself to preserve His own Word, having no need for man. Nevertheless, in the course of God's preservation, which He has been using His churches as His instruments, 'the Law of Inalterability' is a precious God-given opportunity for man's obedience as well as His merciless warning against man's disobedience to His completed and preserved perfect Word. Therefore, all debates related to Verbal Plenary Preservation are from man's 'againstness' to 'the Law of Inalterability,' due to the arrogance of man and all the attempts to arbitrarily alter the Word. In that regard, 'the Law of Inalterability' must be further studied, emphasized, and thoroughly obeyed. As a faithful servant to God's Word, 'the Law of Inalterability' is not an option, but the inevitable and essential virtue for him.

If God directly protects and preserves His Word, and if He does not need any human help in achieving the preservation of the Word, is there no obligation or responsibility for man? No, that is not the case. One clear premise is that when God entrusts His Word to man, it is not intended to rely on man's ability. Man's ability is powerless before the Almighty God, who is omnipotent and everlasting: man is nothing. In fact, man has no power to preserve the truth, the Word of God. The preservation of the Word is entirely through God's supernatural power in His providence. However, the reason why God entrusted man with His Word and commanded him to participate as an instrument in the process of His preservation is that it is a blessing to man; for dwelling with God's eternal truth is the only way for man to be eternally blessed. The writer must clearly point out one fact about the preservation of God's Word, because all the controversies about Verbal Plenary Preservation that have arisen in the Christian academic circle so far is largely from the illusion of who the subject of the preservation of the Word is. This is because man dares to presumptuously confine the subject of preservation to man himself and discuss the impossibility of preservation based on the impossibility of man. But God's Word never says that the subject of preservation is man, because the Subject of preservation is God Himself, the original Author. Therefore, what God demanded of man when He gave His Word is total trust in His Word, that is, faith. And in the full assurance of faith (Heb 10:22), the right mode and attitude that God demands of His children who are honoured to participate in the process of God's preservation of His Word is 'the Law of Inalterability.' Man, especially churches, and theologians and pastors who think they can cut and paste the Word as they like, must remember what this law is: and what is required for man is the absolute obedience to this law of God: 'the Law of Inalterability.'

The newly introduced methodology for the Nestle-Aland 28th edition positively helped this time to get the direction of the changes slightly closer to the *Textus Receptus*, but this result is limited only to the General Epistles, a small portion of the entire New Testament. If the same new methodology is applied to the entire New Testament, it is not predictable at all how the results will be produced. Therefore, if such a methodology is applied to the whole body of the New Testament and a revised edition is republished, it is also necessary to review the types and direction of the changes as a whole compared to the *Textus Receptus*. But the fact that the editors of the Nestle-Aland Greek text have continued repeatedly to edit the text tells a lot about themselves: It means they still do not believe in God's promise of preservation, and in God's Word in which that certain promise is written. And when the cause of their unbelief is traced back to the top, there is eventually their unbelief in God, the Body of the Word of truth. No other excuse is actually needed. So, the reason 'the Law of Inalterability' is disregarded and ignored by them is because of their disrespect and apparent disobedience to God's Word: And eventually it is the disrespect and disobedience to God Himself, the original Author of the written Word. It is not sure how long this pointless editing, where textual changes are made whenever a new methodology comes out, will be repeated. However, this trend will continue as long as they think, without recognizing human limits, that they can restore the Word by themselves with human reason, judgment, and methodologies. Unless they accept God's promise as it is and obey 'the Law of Inalterability' on God's preserved Word (that is, God's strict command and warning about man's essential mode and attitude towards His Word), this tedious and fruitless repetition of their works on the edit treadmill is inevitable, because they do not have the perfect Bible that God has preserved: that is, they have no truth. But their unbelief in the Divine Authority (against Verbal Plenary Preservation) and their resulting disobedience (against 'the Law of Inalterability') foreshadows more serious consequences just beyond that level: it is God's eternal punishment. It is only God's eternal curse that waits those who take lightly the Word of God.

The final prohibition of Revelation 22:18-19, the last book of the Bible, is written in the future conditional clause. And the last verses of Revelation, 22:20-21, end with the imminency of the second coming of Jesus Christ. In other words, this prohibition order of God that was given at the time of the completion of the Bible continues until Jesus

Christ returns and fulfils all the words of the Bible in the future. However, as of the time when Revelation 22:18-19 was written, we are still living in 'that point of the future,' and the second coming of Jesus Christ has not yet been fulfilled. Therefore, 'the Law of Inalterability' is still God's valid command that we must still believe in, firmly hold, and keep.

APPENDIX

[Note]
TR: *Textus Receptus*; NA27: Nestle-Aland 27th Edition; NA28: Nestle-Aland 28th Edition; Diff (27, 28): difference between NA27 and NA28; Diff (TR, 27): difference between TR and NA27; Diff (TR, 28): difference between TR and NA28; Toward TR: corrected toward TR in NA28; Away from TR: corrected away from TR in NA28

Text	TR	NA27	NA28	Diff (27, 28)	Diff (TR, 27)	Diff (TR, 28)	Toward TR	Away from TR
James 1:20	ὀργὴ γὰρ ἀνδρὸς δικαιοσύνην θεοῦ οὐ κατεργάζεται.	ὀργὴ γὰρ ἀνδρὸς δικαιοσύνην θεοῦ οὐκ ἐργάζεται.	ὀργὴ γὰρ ἀνδρὸς δικαιοσύνην θεοῦ οὐ κατεργάζεται.	o	o		o	
James 1:26	εἴ τις δοκεῖ θρησκὸς εἶναι ἐν ὑμῖν, μὴ χαλιναγωγῶν γλῶσσαν αὐτοῦ, ἀλλ' ἀπατῶν καρδίαν αὐτοῦ, τούτου μάταιος ἡ θρησκεία.	Εἴ τις δοκεῖ θρησκὸς εἶναι μὴ χαλιναγωγῶν γλῶσσαν αὐτοῦ ἀλλὰ ἀπατῶν καρδίαν αὐτοῦ, τούτου μάταιος ἡ θρησκεία.	Εἰ τις δοκεῖ θρησκὸς εἶναι μὴ χαλιναγωγῶν γλῶσσαν αὐτοῦ ἀλλ' ἀπατῶν καρδίαν αὐτοῦ, τούτου μάταιος ἡ θρησκεία.	o	o	o	o	
James 2:3	καὶ ἐπιβλέψητε ἐπὶ τὸν φοροῦντα τὴν ἐσθῆτα τὴν λαμπρὰν καὶ εἴπητε αὐτῷ, Σὺ κάθου ὧδε καλῶς, καὶ τῷ πτωχῷ εἴπητε, Σὺ στῆθι ἐκεῖ, ἢ κάθου ὧδε ὑπὸ τὸ ὑποπόδιόν μου·	ἐπιβλέψητε δὲ ἐπὶ τὸν φοροῦντα τὴν ἐσθῆτα τὴν λαμπρὰν καὶ εἴπητε, Σὺ κάθου ὧδε καλῶς, καὶ τῷ πτωχῷ εἴπητε, Σὺ στῆθι ἐκεῖ ἢ κάθου ὑπὸ τὸ ὑποπόδιόν μου,	ἐπιβλέψητε δὲ ἐπὶ τὸν φοροῦντα τὴν ἐσθῆτα τὴν λαμπρὰν καὶ εἴπητε· σὺ κάθου ὧδε καλῶς, καὶ τῷ πτωχῷ εἴπητε· σὺ στῆθι ἐκεῖ ἢ κάθου ἐκεῖ ὑπὸ τὸ ὑποπόδιόν μου,	o	o	o		o
James 2:4	καὶ οὐ διεκρίθητε ἐν ἑαυτοῖς, καὶ ἐγένεσθε κριταὶ διαλογισμῶν πονηρῶν	οὐ διεκρίθητε ἐν ἑαυτοῖς καὶ ἐγένεσθε κριταὶ διαλογισμῶν πονηρῶν	καὶ οὐ διεκρίθητε ἐν ἑαυτοῖς καὶ ἐγένεσθε κριταὶ διαλογισμῶν πονηρῶν;	o	o		o	
James 2:15	ἐὰν δὲ ἀδελφὸς ἢ ἀδελφὴ γυμνοὶ ὑπάρχωσι καὶ λειπόμενοι ὦσι τῆς ἐφημέρου τροφῆς,	ἐὰν ἀδελφὸς ἢ ἀδελφὴ γυμνοὶ ὑπάρχωσιν καὶ λειπόμενοι τῆς ἐφημέρου τροφῆς	ἐὰν ἀδελφὸς ἢ ἀδελφὴ γυμνοὶ ὑπάρχωσιν καὶ λειπόμενοι ὦσιν τῆς ἐφημέρου τροφῆς,	o	o	o	o	
James 3:15	οὐκ ἔστιν αὕτη ἡ σοφία ἄνωθεν κατερχομένη, ἀλλ' ἐπίγειος, ψυχική, δαιμονιώδης.	οὐκ ἔστιν αὕτη ἡ σοφία ἄνωθεν κατερχομένη ἀλλὰ ἐπίγειος, ψυχική, δαιμονιώδης.	οὐκ ἔστιν αὕτη ἡ σοφία ἄνωθεν κατερχομένη ἀλλ' ἐπίγειος, ψυχική, δαιμονιώδης.	o	o		o	
James 4:10	ταπεινώθητε ἐνώπιον τοῦ Κυρίου, καὶ ὑψώσει ὑμᾶς.	ταπεινώθητε ἐνώπιον κυρίου καὶ ὑψώσει ὑμᾶς.	ταπεινώθητε ἐνώπιον τοῦ κυρίου καὶ ὑψώσει ὑμᾶς.	o	o		o	
James 4:12	εἷς ἐστιν ὁ νομοθέτης, ὁ δυνάμενος σῶσαι καὶ ἀπολέσαι· σὺ τίς εἶ ὃς κρίνεις τὸν ἕτερον	εἷς ἐστιν [ὁ] νομοθέτης καὶ κριτής ὁ δυνάμενος σῶσαι καὶ ἀπολέσαι· σὺ δὲ τίς εἶ ὁ κρίνων τὸν πλησίον	εἷς ἐστιν ὁ νομοθέτης καὶ κριτής ὁ δυνάμενος σῶσαι καὶ ἀπολέσαι· σὺ δὲ τίς εἶ ὁ κρίνων τὸν πλησίον;	o	o	o	o	
James 5:14	ἀσθενεῖ τις ἐν ὑμῖν προσκαλεσάσθω τοὺς πρεσβυτέρους τῆς ἐκκλησίας, καὶ προσευξάσθωσαν ἐπ' αὐτόν, ἀλείψαντες αὐτὸν ἐλαίῳ ἐν τῷ ὀνόματι τοῦ Κυρίου·	ἀσθενεῖ τις ἐν ὑμῖν, προσκαλεσάσθω τοὺς πρεσβυτέρους τῆς ἐκκλησίας καὶ προσευξάσθωσαν ἐπ' αὐτὸν ἀλείψαντες [αὐτὸν] ἐλαίῳ ἐν τῷ ὀνόματι τοῦ κυρίου.	ἀσθενεῖ τις ἐν ὑμῖν, προσκαλεσάσθω τοὺς πρεσβυτέρους τῆς ἐκκλησίας καὶ προσευξάσθωσαν ἐπ' αὐτὸν ἀλείψαντες αὐτὸν ἐλαίῳ ἐν τῷ ὀνόματι τοῦ κυρίου.	o	o		o	
1 Peter 1:6	ἐν ᾧ ἀγαλλιᾶσθε ὀλίγον ἄρτι, εἰ δέον ἐστί, λυπηθέντες ἐν ποικίλοις πειρασμοῖς,	ἐν ᾧ ἀγαλλιᾶσθε, ὀλίγον ἄρτι εἰ δέον [ἐστὶν] λυπηθέντες ἐν ποικίλοις πειρασμοῖς,	ἐν ᾧ ἀγαλλιᾶσθε ὀλίγον ἄρτι, εἰ δέον ἐστίν, λυπηθέντας ἐν ποικίλοις πειρασμοῖς,	o	o	o	o	o
1 Peter 1:9	κομιζόμενοι τὸ τέλος τῆς πίστεως ὑμῶν, σωτηρίαν ψυχῶν.	κομιζόμενοι τὸ τέλος τῆς πίστεως [ὑμῶν] σωτηρίαν ψυχῶν.	κομιζόμενοι τὸ τέλος τῆς πίστεως ὑμῶν σωτηρίαν ψυχῶν.	o	o		o	
1 Peter 1:12	οἷς ἀπεκαλύφθη ὅτι οὐχ ἑαυτοῖς, ἡμῖν δὲ διηκόνουν αὐτά, ἃ νῦν ἀνηγγέλη ὑμῖν διὰ τῶν εὐαγγελισαμένων ὑμᾶς ἐν Πνεύματι Ἁγίῳ ἀποσταλέντι ἀπ' οὐρανοῦ, εἰς ἃ ἐπιθυμοῦσιν ἄγγελοι παρακύψαι.	οἷς ἀπεκαλύφθη ὅτι οὐχ ἑαυτοῖς ὑμῖν δὲ διηκόνουν αὐτά, ἃ νῦν ἀνηγγέλη ὑμῖν διὰ τῶν εὐαγγελισαμένων ὑμᾶς [ἐν] πνεύματι ἁγίῳ ἀποσταλέντι ἀπ' οὐρανοῦ, εἰς ἃ ἐπιθυμοῦσιν ἄγγελοι παρακύψαι.	οἷς ἀπεκαλύφθη ὅτι οὐχ ἑαυτοῖς, ὑμῖν δὲ διηκόνουν αὐτὰ ἃ νῦν ἀνηγγέλη ὑμῖν διὰ τῶν εὐαγγελισαμένων ὑμᾶς ἐν πνεύματι ἁγίῳ ἀποσταλέντι ἀπ' οὐρανοῦ, εἰς ἃ ἐπιθυμοῦσιν ἄγγελοι παρακύψαι.	o	o	o	o	
1 Peter 1:16	διότι γέγραπται Ἅγιοι γένεσθε, ὅτι ἐγὼ ἅγιός εἰμι.	διότι γέγραπται [ὅτι] Ἅγιοι ἔσεσθε, ὅτι ἐγὼ ἅγιος [εἰμι]	διότι γέγραπται· ἅγιοι ἔσεσθε, ὅτι ἐγὼ ἅγιος.	o	o	o	o	o

(P.T.O.)

Text	TR	NA27	NA28	Diff (27, 28)	Diff (TR, 27)	Diff (TR, 28)	Toward TR	Away from TR
1 Peter 1:22	τὰς ψυχὰς ὑμῶν ἡγνικότες ἐν τῇ ὑπακοῇ τῆς ἀληθείας διὰ Πνεύματος εἰς φιλαδελφίαν ἀνυπόκριτον, ἐκ καθαρᾶς καρδίας ἀλλήλους ἀγαπήσατε ἐκτενῶς.	Τὰς ψυχὰς ὑμῶν ἡγνικότες ἐν τῇ ὑπακοῇ τῆς ἀληθείας εἰς φιλαδελφίαν ἀνυπόκριτον, ἐκ [καθαρᾶς] καρδίας ἀλλήλους ἀγαπήσατε ἐκτενῶς	Τὰς ψυχὰς ὑμῶν ἡγνικότες ἐν τῇ ὑπακοῇ τῆς ἀληθείας εἰς φιλαδελφίαν ἀνυπόκριτον ἐκ καθαρᾶς καρδίας ἀλλήλους ἀγαπήσατε ἐκτενῶς	○	○	○	○	
1 Peter 1:23	ἀναγεγεννημένοι οὐκ ἐκ σπορᾶς φθαρτῆς, ἀλλὰ ἀφθάρτου, διὰ λόγου ζῶντος Θεοῦ καὶ μένοντος εἰς τὸν αἰῶνα.	ἀναγεγεννημένοι οὐκ ἐκ σπορᾶς φθαρτῆς ἀλλὰ ἀφθάρτου διὰ λόγου ζῶντος θεοῦ καὶ μένοντος.	ἀναγεγεννημένοι οὐκ ἐκ σπορᾶς φθαρτῆς ἀλλ' ἀφθάρτου διὰ λόγου ζῶντος θεοῦ καὶ μένοντος.	○	○	○		○
1 Peter 2:5	καὶ αὐτοὶ ὡς λίθοι ζῶντες οἰκοδομεῖσθε οἶκος πνευματικὸς, ἱεράτευμα ἅγιον, ἀνενέγκαι πνευματικὰς θυσίας εὐπροσδέκτους τῷ Θεῷ διὰ Ἰησοῦ Χριστοῦ.	καὶ αὐτοὶ ὡς λίθοι ζῶντες οἰκοδομεῖσθε οἶκος πνευματικὸς εἰς ἱεράτευμα ἅγιον ἀνενέγκαι πνευματικὰς θυσίας εὐπροσδέκτους [τῷ] θεῷ διὰ Ἰησοῦ Χριστοῦ.	καὶ αὐτοὶ ὡς λίθοι ζῶντες οἰκοδομεῖσθε οἶκος πνευματικὸς εἰς ἱεράτευμα ἅγιον ἀνενέγκαι πνευματικὰς θυσίας εὐπροσδέκτους θεῷ διὰ Ἰησοῦ Χριστοῦ.	○	○	○		○
1 Peter 2:25	ἦτε γὰρ ὡς πρόβατα πλανώμενα· ἀλλ' ἐπεστράφητε νῦν ἐπὶ τὸν ποιμένα καὶ ἐπίσκοπον τῶν ψυχῶν ὑμῶν.	ἦτε γὰρ ὡς πρόβατα πλανώμενοι, ἀλλὰ ἐπεστράφητε νῦν ἐπὶ τὸν ποιμένα καὶ ἐπίσκοπον τῶν ψυχῶν ὑμῶν.	ἦτε γὰρ ὡς πρόβατα πλανώμενοι, ἀλλ' ἐπεστράφητε νῦν ἐπὶ τὸν ποιμένα καὶ ἐπίσκοπον τῶν ψυχῶν ὑμῶν.	○	○	○	○	
1 Peter 3:1	Ὁμοίως, αἱ γυναῖκες ὑποτασσόμεναι τοῖς ἰδίοις ἀνδράσιν, ἵνα καὶ εἴ τινες ἀπειθοῦσι τῷ λόγῳ, διὰ τῆς τῶν γυναικῶν ἀναστροφῆς ἄνευ λόγου κερδηθήσωνται	Ὁμοίως [αἱ] γυναῖκες, ὑποτασσόμεναι τοῖς ἰδίοις ἀνδράσιν, ἵνα καὶ εἴ τινες ἀπειθοῦσιν τῷ λόγῳ, διὰ τῆς τῶν γυναικῶν ἀναστροφῆς ἄνευ λόγου κερδηθήσονται,	ὁμοίως αἱ γυναῖκες, ὑποτασσόμεναι τοῖς ἰδίοις ἀνδράσιν, ἵνα καὶ εἴ τινες ἀπειθοῦσιν τῷ λόγῳ, διὰ τῆς τῶν γυναικῶν ἀναστροφῆς ἄνευ λόγου κερδηθήσονται	○	○	○	○	
1 Peter 3:22	ὅς ἐστιν ἐν δεξιᾷ τοῦ Θεοῦ, πορευθεὶς εἰς οὐρανόν, ὑποταγέντων αὐτῷ ἀγγέλων καὶ ἐξουσιῶν καὶ δυνάμεων.	ὅς ἐστιν ἐν δεξιᾷ [τοῦ] θεοῦ πορευθεὶς εἰς οὐρανόν ὑποταγέντων αὐτῷ ἀγγέλων καὶ ἐξουσιῶν καὶ δυνάμεων.	ὅς ἐστιν ἐν δεξιᾷ τοῦ θεοῦ πορευθεὶς εἰς οὐρανὸν ὑποταγέντων αὐτῷ ἀγγέλων καὶ ἐξουσιῶν καὶ δυνάμεων.	○	○		○	
1 Peter 4:16	εἰ δὲ ὡς Χριστιανός, μὴ αἰσχυνέσθω, δοξαζέτω δὲ τὸν Θεὸν ἐν τῷ μέρει τούτῳ.	εἰ δὲ ὡς Χριστιανός, μὴ αἰσχυνέσθω, δοξαζέτω δὲ τὸν θεὸν ἐν τῷ ὀνόματι τούτῳ.	εἰ δὲ ὡς χριστιανός, μὴ αἰσχυνέσθω, δοξαζέτω δὲ τὸν θεὸν ἐν τῷ μέρει τούτῳ.	○	○		○	
1 Peter 4:17	ὅτι ὁ καιρὸς τοῦ ἄρξασθαι τὸ κρίμα ἀπὸ τοῦ οἴκου τοῦ Θεοῦ· εἰ δὲ πρῶτον ἀφ' ἡμῶν, τί τὸ τέλος τῶν ἀπειθούντων τῷ τοῦ Θεοῦ εὐαγγελίῳ	ὅτι [ὁ] καιρὸς τοῦ ἄρξασθαι τὸ κρίμα ἀπὸ τοῦ οἴκου τοῦ θεοῦ· εἰ δὲ πρῶτον ἀφ' ἡμῶν, τί τὸ τέλος τῶν ἀπειθούντων τῷ τοῦ θεοῦ εὐαγγελίῳ	ὅτι ὁ καιρὸς τοῦ ἄρξασθαι τὸ κρίμα ἀπὸ τοῦ οἴκου τοῦ θεοῦ· εἰ δὲ πρῶτον ἀφ' ἡμῶν, τί τὸ τέλος τῶν ἀπειθούντων τῷ τοῦ θεοῦ εὐαγγελίῳ;	○	○		○	
1 Peter 5:1	Πρεσβυτέρους τοὺς ἐν ὑμῖν παρακαλῶ ὁ συμπρεσβύτερος καὶ μάρτυς τῶν τοῦ Χριστοῦ παθημάτων, ὁ καὶ τῆς μελλούσης ἀποκαλύπτεσθαι δόξης κοινωνός·	Πρεσβυτέρους οὖν ἐν ὑμῖν παρακαλῶ ὁ συμπρεσβύτερος καὶ μάρτυς τῶν τοῦ Χριστοῦ παθημάτων, ὁ καὶ τῆς μελλούσης ἀποκαλύπτεσθαι δόξης κοινωνός·	Πρεσβυτέρους τοὺς ἐν ὑμῖν παρακαλῶ ὁ συμπρεσβύτερος καὶ μάρτυς τῶν τοῦ Χριστοῦ παθημάτων, ὁ καὶ τῆς μελλούσης ἀποκαλύπτεσθαι δόξης κοινωνός·	○	○		○	
1 Peter 5:2	ποιμάνατε τὸ ἐν ὑμῖν ποίμνιον τοῦ Θεοῦ, ἐπισκοποῦντες μὴ ἀναγκαστῶς, ἀλλ' ἑκουσίως· μηδὲ αἰσχροκερδῶς, ἀλλὰ προθύμως,	ποιμάνατε τὸ ἐν ὑμῖν ποίμνιον τοῦ θεοῦ [ἐπισκοποῦντες] μὴ ἀναγκαστῶς ἀλλὰ ἑκουσίως κατὰ θεόν, μηδὲ αἰσχροκερδῶς ἀλλὰ προθύμως,	ποιμάνατε τὸ ἐν ὑμῖν ποίμνιον τοῦ θεοῦ ἐπισκοποῦντες μὴ ἀναγκαστῶς ἀλλ' ἑκουσίως κατὰ θεόν, μηδὲ αἰσχροκερδῶς ἀλλὰ προθύμως,	○	○	○	○	
1 Peter 5:5	ὁμοίως, νεώτεροι, ὑποτάγητε πρεσβυτέροις· πάντες δὲ ἀλλήλοις ὑποτασσόμενοι, τὴν ταπεινοφροσύνην ἐγκομβώσασθε· ὅτι ὁ Θεὸς ὑπερηφάνοις ἀντιτάσσεται, ταπεινοῖς δὲ δίδωσι χάριν.	Ὁμοίως, νεώτεροι, ὑποτάγητε πρεσβυτέροις· πάντες δὲ ἀλλήλοις τὴν ταπεινοφροσύνην ἐγκομβώσασθε, ὅτι [ὁ] θεὸς ὑπερηφάνοις ἀντιτάσσεται, ταπεινοῖς δὲ δίδωσιν χάριν.	ὁμοίως, νεώτεροι, ὑποτάγητε πρεσβυτέροις· πάντες δὲ ἀλλήλοις τὴν ταπεινοφροσύνην ἐγκομβώσασθε, ὅτι ὁ θεὸς ὑπερηφάνοις ἀντιτάσσεται, ταπεινοῖς δὲ δίδωσιν χάριν.	○	○	○	○	

(P.T.O.)

Text	TR	NA27	NA28	Diff (27, 28)	Diff (TR, 27)	Diff (TR, 28)	Toward TR	Away from TR
1 Peter 5:8	νήψατε, γρηγορήσατε, ὅτι ὁ ἀντίδικος ὑμῶν διάβολος, ὡς λέων ὡ ρυόμενος περιπατεῖ ζ ητῶν τινα καταπίῃ·	Νήψατε, γρηγορήσατε . ὁ ἀντίδικος ὑμῶν δι άβολος ὡς λέων ὠρυό μενος περιπατεῖ ζητῶ ν [τινα] καταπιεῖν·	νήψατε, γρηγορήσατε. ὁ ἀντίδικος ὑμῶν διάβολος ὡς λέων ὠρυόμενος περιπατεῖ ζητῶν τινα καταπιεῖν·	o	o	o	o	
1 Peter 5:9	ᾧ ἀντίστητε στερεοὶ τῇ πίστει, εἰδότες τὰ αὐτὰ τῶν παθημάτων τῇ ἐν κόσμῳ ὑμῶν ἀ δελφότητι ἐπιτελεῖσθ αι.	ᾧ ἀντίστητε στερεοὶ τῇ πίστει εἰδότες τὰ αὐτὰ τῶν παθημάτων τῇ ἐν [τῷ] κόσμῳ ὑμ ῶν ἀδελφότητι ἐπιτελ εῖσθαι.	ᾧ ἀντίστητε στερεοὶ τῇ πίστει εἰδότες τὰ αὐτὰ τῶν παθημάτων τῇ ἐν κόσμῳ ὑμῶν ἀδελφότητι ἐπιτελεῖσθαι.	o	o		o	
1 Peter 5:10	ὁ δὲ θεὸς πάσης χάρι τος, ὁ καλέσας ἡμᾶς εἰς τὴν αἰώνιον αὐτοῦ δόξαν ἐν Χριστῷ Ἰησ οῦ, ὀλίγον παθόντας αὐτὸς καταρτίσαι ὑμᾶ ς, στηρίξαι, σθενῶσαι, θεμελιῶσαι.	Ὁ δὲ θεὸς πάσης χάρ ιτος, ὁ καλέσας ὑμᾶς εἰς τὴν αἰώνιον αὐτο ῦ δόξαν ἐν Χριστῷ ((Ἰι ησοῦ)), ὀλίγον παθόντ ας αὐτὸς καταρτίσει, στηρίξει, σθενώσει, θε μελιώσει.	ὁ δὲ θεὸς πάσης χάριτος, ὁ καλέσας ὑμᾶς εἰς τὴν αἰώνιον αὐτοῦ δόξαν ἐν Χριστῷ ὀλίγον παθόντας αὐτὸς καταρτίσει, στηρίξει, σθενώσει, θεμελιώσει.	o	o	o		o
2 Peter 1:21	οὐ γὰρ θελήματι ἀνθρ ώπου ἠνέχθη ποτέ πρ οφητεία, ἀλλ' ὑπὸ Πν εύματος Ἁγίου φερό μενοι ἐλάλησαν ἅγιοι Θεοῦ ἄνθρωποι.	οὐ γὰρ θελήματι ἀνθρ ώπου ἠνέχθη προφητε ία ποτέ, ἀλλὰ ὑπὸ πν εύματος ἁγίου φερόμε νοι ἐλάλησαν ἀπὸ θεο ῦ ἄνθρωποι.	οὐ γὰρ θελήματι ἀνθρώπου ἠνέχθη προφητεία ποτέ, ἀλλ' ὑπὸ πνεύματος ἁγίου φερόμενοι ἐλάλησαν ἀπὸ θεοῦ ἄνθρωποι	o	o	o	o	
2 Peter 2:5	καὶ ἀρχαίου κόσμου ο ὐκ ἐφείσατο, ἀλλ' ὄγδ οον Νῶε δικαιοσύνης κήρυκα ἐφύλαξε, κατα κλυσμὸν κόσμῳ ἀσεβῶ ν ἐπάξας·	καὶ ἀρχαίου κόσμου ο ὐκ ἐφείσατο ἀλλὰ ὄγδ οον Νῶε δικαιοσύνης κήρυκα ἐφύλαξεν κατα κλυσμὸν κόσμῳ ἀσεβῶ ν ἐπάξας,	καὶ ἀρχαίου κόσμου οὐκ ἐφείσατο ἀλλ' ὄγδοον Νῶε δικαιοσύνης κήρυκα ἐφύλαξεν κατακλυσμὸν κόσμῳ ἀσεβῶν ἐπάξας	o	o		o	
2 Peter 2:6	καὶ πόλεις Σοδόμων κ αὶ Γομόρρας τεφρώσα ς καταστροφῇ κατέκρ ινεν, ὑπόδειγμα μελλό ντων ἀσεβεῖν τεθεικώ ς·	καὶ πόλεις Σοδόμων κ αὶ Γομόρρας τεφρώσα ς [καταστροφῇ] κατέ κρινεν ὑπόδειγμα μελ λόντων ἀσεβέ[σ]ιν τε θεικώς,	καὶ πόλεις Σοδόμων καὶ Γομόρρας τεφρώσας καταστροφῇ κατέκρινεν ὑπόδειγμα μελλόντων ἀσεβεῖν τεθεικὼς	o	o		o	
2 Peter 2:11	ὅπου ἄγγελοι, ἰσχύϊ κ αὶ δυνάμει μείζονες ὄ ντες, οὐ φέρουσι κατ' αὐτῶν παρὰ Κυρίῳ β λάσφημον κρίσιν.	ὅπου ἄγγελοι ἰσχύϊ κ αὶ δυνάμει μείζονες ὄ ντες οὐ φέρουσιν κατ' αὐτῶν παρὰ κυρίου β λάσφημον κρίσιν.	ὅπου ἄγγελοι ἰσχύϊ καὶ δυνάμει μείζονες ὄντες οὐ φέρουσιν κατ' αὐτῶν παρὰ κυρίῳ βλάσφημον κρίσιν.	o	o		o	
2 Peter 2:15	καταλίποντες τὴν εὐθ εῖαν ὁδὸν ἐπλανήθησα ν, ἐξακολουθήσαντες τῇ ὁδῷ τοῦ Βαλαὰμ τ οῦ Βοσόρ, ὃς μισθὸν ἀ δικίας ἠγάπησεν,	καταλείποντες εὐθεῖα ν ὁδὸν ἐπλανήθησαν, ἐξακολουθήσαντες τῇ ὁδῷ τοῦ Βαλαὰμ τοῦ Βοσόρ, ὃς μισθὸν ἀδικ ίας ἠγάπησεν	καταλιπόντες εὐθεῖαν ὁδὸν ἐπλανήθησαν ἐξακολουθήσαντες τῇ ὁδῷ τοῦ Βαλαὰμ τοῦ Βοσὸρ ὃς μισθὸν ἀδικίας ἠγάπησεν,	o	o	o	o	
2 Peter 2:18	ὑπέρογκα γὰρ ματαιό τητος φθεγγόμενοι, δ ελεάζουσιν ἐν ἐπιθυμί αις σαρκὸς ἐν ἀσελγε ίαις, τοὺς ὄντως ἀπο φύγοντας τοὺς ἐν πλ άνῃ ἀναστρεφομένους,	ὑπέρογκα γὰρ ματαιό τητος φθεγγόμενοι δε λεάζουσιν ἐν ἐπιθυμία ις σαρκὸς ἀσελγείαις τοὺς ὀλίγως ἀποφεύγ οντας τοὺς ἐν πλάνῃ ἀναστρεφομένους,	ὑπέρογκα γὰρ ματαιότητος φθεγγόμενοι δελεάζουσιν ἐν ἐπιθυμίαις σαρκὸς ἀσελγείαις τοὺς ὄντως ἀποφεύγοντας τοὺς ἐν πλάνῃ ἀναστρεφομένους,	o	o	o	o	
2 Peter 2:20	εἰ γὰρ ἀποφυγόντες τ ὰ μιάσματα τοῦ κόσμ ου ἐν ἐπιγνώσει τοῦ Κυρίου καὶ σωτῆρος Ἰ ησοῦ Χριστοῦ, τούτοι ς δὲ πάλιν ἐμπλακέντ ες ἡττῶνται, γέγονεν αὐτοῖς τὰ ἔσχατα χε ίρονα τῶν πρώτων.	εἰ γὰρ ἀποφυγόντες τ ὰ μιάσματα τοῦ κόσμ ου ἐν ἐπιγνώσει τοῦ κυρίου [ἡμῶν] καὶ σω τῆρος Ἰησοῦ Χριστοῦ, τούτοις δὲ πάλιν ἐμ πλακέντες ἡττῶνται, γέγονεν αὐτοῖς τὰ ἔσ χατα χείρονα τῶν πρ ώτων.	εἰ γὰρ ἀποφυγόντες τὰ μιάσματα τοῦ κόσμου ἐν ἐπιγνώσει τοῦ κυρίου καὶ σωτῆρος Ἰησοῦ Χριστοῦ, τούτοις δὲ πάλιν ἐμπλακέντες ἡττῶνται, γέγονεν αὐτοῖς τὰ ἔσχατα χείρονα τῶν πρώτων.	o	o		o	
2 Peter 3:6	δι' ὧν ὁ τότε κόσμος ὕδατι κατακλυσθεὶς ἀ πώλετο·	δι' ὧν ὁ τότε κόσμος ὕδατι κατακλυσθεὶς ἀ πώλετο·	δι' ὃν ὁ τότε κόσμος ὕδατι κατακλυσθεὶς ἀπώλετο·	o		o		o
2 Peter 3:10	ἥξει δὲ ἡ ἡμέρα Κυρί ου ὡς κλέπτης ἐν νυκ τί, ἐν ᾗ οἱ οὐρανοὶ ρο ιζηδὸν παρελεύσονται, στοιχεῖα δὲ καυσούμ ενα λυθήσονται, καὶ γ ῆ καὶ τὰ ἐν αὐτῇ ἔργ α κατακαήσεται.	Ἥξει δὲ ἡμέρα κυρίου ὡς κλέπτης, ἐν ᾗ οἱ οὐρανοὶ ῥοιζηδὸν παρ ελεύσονται στοιχεῖα δὲ καυσούμενα λυθήσε ται καὶ γῆ καὶ τὰ ἐν αὐτῇ ἔργα εὑρεθήσετ αι.	Ἥξει δὲ ἡμέρα κυρίου ὡς κλέπτης ἐν ᾗ οἱ οὐρανοὶ ῥοιζηδὸν παρελεύσονται, στοιχεῖα δὲ καυσούμενα λυθήσεται καὶ γῆ καὶ τὰ ἐν αὐτῇ ἔργα οὐχ εὑρεθήσεται.	o	o	o		o

(P.T.O.)

Text	TR	NA27	NA28	Diff (27, 28)	Diff (TR, 27)	Diff (TR, 28)	Toward TR	Away from TR
2 Peter 3:11	τούτων <u>οὖν</u> πάντων λυομένων, ποταποὺς δεῖ ὑπάρχειν <u>ὑμᾶς</u> ἐν ἁγίαις ἀναστροφαῖς καὶ εὐσεβείαις,	τούτων <u>οὕτως</u> πάντων λυομένων ποταποὺς δεῖ ὑπάρχειν <u>[ὑμᾶς]</u> ἐν ἁγίαις ἀναστροφαῖς καὶ εὐσεβείαις,	Τούτων <u>οὕτως</u> πάντων λυομένων ποταποὺς δεῖ ὑπάρχειν <u>ὑμᾶς</u> ἐν ἁγίαις ἀναστροφαῖς καὶ εὐσεβείαις	○	○	○	○	
2 Peter 3:16	ὡς καὶ ἐν πάσαις <u>ταῖς ἐπιστολαῖς</u>, λαλῶν ἐν αὐταῖς περὶ τούτων, ἐν οἷς ἐστι δυσνόητά τινα, ἃ οἱ ἀμαθεῖς καὶ ἀστήρικτοι <u>στρεβλοῦσιν</u>, ὡς καὶ τὰς λοιπὰς γραφὰς, πρὸς τὴν ἰδίαν αὐτῶν ἀπώλειαν.	ὡς καὶ ἐν πάσαις <u>ἐπιστολαῖς</u> λαλῶν ἐν αὐταῖς περὶ τούτων, ἐν αἷς ἐστιν δυσνόητά τινα, ἃ οἱ ἀμαθεῖς καὶ ἀστήρικτοι <u>στρεβλοῦσιν</u> ὡς καὶ τὰς λοιπὰς γραφὰς πρὸς τὴν ἰδίαν αὐτῶν ἀπώλειαν.	ὡς καὶ ἐν πάσαις <u>ταῖς ἐπιστολαῖς</u> λαλῶν ἐν αὐταῖς περὶ τούτων ἐν αἷς ἐστιν δυσνόητά τινα ἃ οἱ ἀμαθεῖς καὶ ἀστήρικτοι <u>στρεβλώσουσιν</u> ὡς καὶ τὰς λοιπὰς γραφὰς πρὸς τὴν ἰδίαν αὐτῶν ἀπώλειαν.	○	○	○	○	○
2 Peter 3:18	αὐξάνετε δὲ ἐν χάριτι καὶ γνώσει τοῦ Κυρίου ἡμῶν καὶ σωτῆρος Ἰησοῦ Χριστοῦ. αὐτῷ ἡ δόξα καὶ νῦν καὶ εἰς ἡμέραν αἰῶνος. <u>ἀμήν.</u>	αὐξάνετε δὲ ἐν χάριτι καὶ γνώσει τοῦ κυρίου ἡμῶν καὶ σωτῆρος Ἰησοῦ Χριστοῦ. αὐτῷ ἡ δόξα καὶ νῦν καὶ εἰς ἡμέραν αἰῶνος. <u>[ἀμήν.]</u>	αὐξάνετε δὲ ἐν χάριτι καὶ γνώσει τοῦ κυρίου ἡμῶν καὶ σωτῆρος Ἰησοῦ Χριστοῦ. αὐτῷ ἡ δόξα καὶ νῦν καὶ εἰς ἡμέραν αἰῶνος.	○	○	○		○
1 John 1:7	ἐὰν <u>δὲ</u> ἐν τῷ φωτὶ περιπατῶμεν, ὡς αὐτός ἐστιν ἐν τῷ φωτί, κοινωνίαν ἔχομεν μετ' ἀλλήλων, καὶ τὸ αἷμα Ἰησοῦ <u>Χριστοῦ</u> τοῦ υἱοῦ αὐτοῦ καθαρίζει ἡμᾶς ἀπὸ πάσης ἁμαρτίας.	ἐὰν <u>δὲ</u> ἐν τῷ φωτὶ περιπατῶμεν ὡς αὐτός ἐστιν ἐν τῷ φωτί, κοινωνίαν ἔχομεν μετ' ἀλλήλων καὶ τὸ αἷμα Ἰησοῦ τοῦ υἱοῦ αὐτοῦ καθαρίζει ἡμᾶς ἀπὸ πάσης ἁμαρτίας.	ἐὰν ἐν τῷ φωτὶ περιπατῶμεν, ὡς αὐτός ἐστιν ἐν τῷ φωτί, κοινωνίαν ἔχομεν μετ' ἀλλήλων, καὶ τὸ αἷμα Ἰησοῦ τοῦ υἱοῦ αὐτοῦ καθαρίζει ἡμᾶς ἀπὸ πάσης ἁμαρτίας.	○	○	○		○
1 John 2:6	ὁ λέγων ἐν αὐτῷ μένειν ὀφείλει, καθὼς ἐκεῖνος περιεπάτησε, καὶ αὐτὸς <u>οὕτω</u> περιπατεῖν.	ὁ λέγων ἐν αὐτῷ μένειν ὀφείλει καθὼς ἐκεῖνος περιεπάτησεν καὶ αὐτὸς <u>[οὕτως]</u> περιπατεῖν.	ὁ λέγων ἐν αὐτῷ μένειν ὀφείλει, καθὼς ἐκεῖνος περιεπάτησεν, καὶ αὐτὸς <u>οὕτως</u> περιπατεῖν.	○	○		○	
1 John 3:7	<u>τεκνία</u>, μηδεὶς πλανάτω ὑμᾶς· ὁ ποιῶν τὴν δικαιοσύνην δίκαιός ἐστι, καθὼς ἐκεῖνος δίκαιός ἐστιν·	<u>Τεκνία</u>, μηδεὶς πλανάτω ὑμᾶς· ὁ ποιῶν τὴν δικαιοσύνην δίκαιός ἐστιν, καθὼς ἐκεῖνος δίκαιός ἐστιν·	<u>Παιδία</u>, μηδεὶς πλανάτω ὑμᾶς· ὁ ποιῶν τὴν δικαιοσύνην δίκαιός ἐστιν, καθὼς ἐκεῖνος δίκαιός ἐστιν·	○		○		○
1 John 3:18	τεκνία <u>μου</u>, μὴ ἀγαπῶμεν λόγῳ μηδὲ γλώσσῃ, <u>ἀλλ'</u> ἔργῳ καὶ ἀληθείᾳ.	Τεκνία, μὴ ἀγαπῶμεν λόγῳ μηδὲ <u>τῇ</u> γλώσσῃ <u>ἀλλὰ</u> ἐν ἔργῳ καὶ ἀληθείᾳ.	Τεκνία, μὴ ἀγαπῶμεν λόγῳ μηδὲ <u>τῇ</u> γλώσσῃ, <u>ἀλλ'</u> ἐν ἔργῳ καὶ ἀληθείᾳ,	○	○	○	○	
1 John 3:19	<u>καὶ</u> ἐν τούτῳ <u>γινώσκομεν</u> ὅτι ἐκ τῆς ἀληθείας ἐσμέν, καὶ ἔμπροσθεν αὐτοῦ πείσομεν <u>τὰς καρδίας</u> ἡμῶν,	<u>[καὶ]</u> ἐν τούτῳ <u>γνωσόμεθα</u> ὅτι ἐκ τῆς ἀληθείας ἐσμέν, καὶ ἔμπροσθεν αὐτοῦ πείσομεν <u>τὴν καρδίαν</u> ἡμῶν,	Καὶ ἐν τούτῳ <u>γνωσόμεθα</u> ὅτι ἐκ τῆς ἀληθείας ἐσμέν. καὶ ἔμπροσθεν αὐτοῦ πείσομεν <u>τὴν καρδίαν</u> ἡμῶν,	○	○	○	○	
1 John 3:21	ἀγαπητοί, ἐὰν ἡ καρδία <u>ἡμῶν</u> μὴ καταγινώσκῃ <u>ἡμῶν</u>, παρρησίαν ἔχομεν πρὸς τὸν Θεόν,	Ἀγαπητοί, ἐὰν ἡ καρδία <u>[ἡμῶν]</u> μὴ καταγινώσκῃ, παρρησίαν ἔχομεν πρὸς τὸν θεόν	Ἀγαπητοί, ἐὰν ἡ καρδία <u>ἡμῶν</u> μὴ καταγινώσκῃ, παρρησίαν ἔχομεν πρὸς τὸν θεόν	○	○	○	○	
1 John 5:1	Πᾶς ὁ πιστεύων ὅτι Ἰησοῦς ἐστιν ὁ Χριστὸς ἐκ τοῦ Θεοῦ γεγέννηται· καὶ πᾶς ὁ ἀγαπῶν τὸν γεννήσαντα ἀγαπᾷ <u>καὶ</u> τὸν γεγεννημένον ἐξ αὐτοῦ.	Πᾶς ὁ πιστεύων ὅτι Ἰησοῦς ἐστιν ὁ Χριστὸς, ἐκ τοῦ θεοῦ γεγέννηται, καὶ πᾶς ὁ ἀγαπῶν τὸν γεννήσαντα ἀγαπᾷ <u>[καὶ]</u> τὸν γεγεννημένον ἐξ αὐτοῦ.	Πᾶς ὁ πιστεύων ὅτι Ἰησοῦς ἐστιν ὁ Χριστὸς ἐκ τοῦ θεοῦ γεγέννηται, καὶ πᾶς ὁ ἀγαπῶν τὸν γεννήσαντα ἀγαπᾷ <u>καὶ</u> τὸν γεγεννημένον ἐξ αὐτοῦ.	○	○		○	
1 John 5:10	ὁ πιστεύων εἰς τὸν υἱὸν τοῦ Θεοῦ ἔχει τὴν μαρτυρίαν <u>ἐν ἑαυτῷ·</u> ὁ μὴ πιστεύων τῷ Θεῷ, ψεύστην πεποίηκεν αὐτόν, ὅτι οὐ πεπίστευκεν εἰς τὴν μαρτυρίαν, ἣν μεμαρτύρηκεν ὁ Θεὸς περὶ τοῦ υἱοῦ αὐτοῦ.	ὁ πιστεύων εἰς τὸν υἱὸν τοῦ θεοῦ ἔχει τὴν μαρτυρίαν <u>ἐν ἑαυτῷ,</u> ὁ μὴ πιστεύων τῷ θεῷ ψεύστην πεποίηκεν αὐτόν, ὅτι οὐ πεπίστευκεν εἰς τὴν μαρτυρίαν ἣν μεμαρτύρηκεν ὁ θεὸς περὶ τοῦ υἱοῦ αὐτοῦ.	ὁ πιστεύων εἰς τὸν υἱὸν τοῦ θεοῦ ἔχει τὴν μαρτυρίαν <u>ἐν αὐτῷ,</u> ὁ μὴ πιστεύων τῷ θεῷ ψεύστην πεποίηκεν αὐτόν, ὅτι οὐ πεπίστευκεν εἰς τὴν μαρτυρίαν ἣν μεμαρτύρηκεν ὁ θεὸς περὶ τοῦ υἱοῦ αὐτοῦ.	○		○		○

(P.T.O.)

Text	TR	NA27	NA28	Diff (27, 28)	Diff (TR, 27)	Diff (TR, 28)	Toward TR	Away from TR
1 John 5:18	Οἴδαμεν ὅτι πᾶς ὁ γεννημένος ἐκ τοῦ Θεοῦ οὐχ ἁμαρτάνει· ἀλλ' ὁ γεννηθεὶς ἐκ τοῦ Θεοῦ τηρεῖ ἑαυτὸν, καὶ ὁ πονηρὸς οὐχ ἅπτεται αὐτοῦ.	Οἴδαμεν ὅτι πᾶς ὁ γεννημένος ἐκ τοῦ θεοῦ οὐχ ἁμαρτάνει, ἀλλ' ὁ γεννηθεὶς ἐκ τοῦ θεοῦ τηρεῖ αὐτὸν καὶ ὁ πονηρὸς οὐχ ἅπτεται αὐτοῦ.	Οἴδαμεν ὅτι πᾶς ὁ γεγεννημένος ἐκ τοῦ θεοῦ οὐχ ἁμαρτάνει, ἀλλ' ὁ γεννηθεὶς ἐκ τοῦ θεοῦ τηρεῖ ἑαυτὸν καὶ ὁ πονηρὸς οὐχ ἅπτεται αὐτοῦ.	o	o		o	
2 John 5	καὶ νῦν ἐρωτῶ σε, κυρία, οὐχ ὡς ἐντολὴν γράφων σοι καινήν, ἀλλὰ ἣν εἴχομεν ἀπ' ἀρχῆς, ἵνα ἀγαπῶμεν ἀλλήλους.	καὶ νῦν ἐρωτῶ σε, κυρία, οὐχ ὡς ἐντολὴν καινὴν γράφων σοι ἀλλὰ ἣν εἴχομεν ἀπ' ἀρχῆς, ἵνα ἀγαπῶμεν ἀλλήλους.	καὶ νῦν ἐρωτῶ σε, κυρία, οὐχ ὡς ἐντολὴν γράφων σοι καινὴν ἀλλ' ἣν εἴχομεν ἀπ' ἀρχῆς, ἵνα ἀγαπῶμεν ἀλλήλους.	o	o		o	
2 John 12	Πολλὰ ἔχων ὑμῖν γράφειν, οὐκ ἠβουλήθην διὰ χάρτου καὶ μέλανος· ἀλλὰ ἐλπίζω ἐλθεῖν πρὸς ὑμᾶς, καὶ στόμα πρὸς στόμα λαλῆσαι, ἵνα ἡ χαρὰ ἡμῶν ᾖ πεπληρωμένη.	Πολλὰ ἔχων ὑμῖν γράφειν οὐκ ἐβουλήθην διὰ χάρτου καὶ μέλανος, ἀλλὰ ἐλπίζω γενέσθαι πρὸς ὑμᾶς καὶ στόμα πρὸς στόμα λαλῆσαι, ἵνα ἡ χαρὰ ἡμῶν πεπληρωμένη ᾖ.	Πολλὰ ἔχων ὑμῖν γράφειν οὐκ ἐβουλήθην διὰ χάρτου καὶ μέλανος, ἀλλ' ἐλπίζω γενέσθαι πρὸς ὑμᾶς καὶ στόμα πρὸς στόμα λαλῆσαι, ἵνα ἡ χαρὰ ἡμῶν ᾖ πεπληρωμένη.	o	o	o	o	
3 John 4	μειζοτέραν τούτων οὐκ ἔχω χαράν, ἵνα ἀκούω τὰ ἐμὰ τέκνα ἐν ἀληθείᾳ περιπατοῦντα.	μειζοτέραν τούτων οὐκ ἔχω χαράν, ἵνα ἀκούω τὰ ἐμὰ τέκνα ἐν τῇ ἀληθείᾳ περιπατοῦντα.	μειζοτέραν τούτων οὐκ ἔχω χαράν, ἵνα ἀκούω τὰ ἐμὰ τέκνα ἐν ἀληθείᾳ περιπατοῦντα.	o	o		o	
Jude 5	Ὑπομνῆσαι δὲ ὑμᾶς βούλομαι, εἰδότας ὑμᾶς ἅπαξ τοῦτο, ὅτι ὁ Κύριος, λαὸν ἐκ γῆς Αἰγύπτου σώσας, τὸ δεύτερον τοὺς μὴ πιστεύσαντας ἀπώλεσεν.	Ὑπομνῆσαι δὲ ὑμᾶς βούλομαι, εἰδότας ((ὑμᾶς)) πάντα ὅτι ((ὁ)) κύριος ἅπαξ λαὸν ἐκ γῆς Αἰγύπτου σώσας τὸ δεύτερον τοὺς μὴ πιστεύσαντας ἀπώλεσεν,	ὑπομνῆσαι δὲ ὑμᾶς βούλομαι, εἰδότας ὑμᾶς ἅπαξ πάντα ὅτι Ἰησοῦς λαὸν ἐκ γῆς Αἰγύπτου σώσας τὸ δεύτερον τοὺς μὴ πιστεύσαντας ἀπώλεσεν,	o	o	o	o	o
Jude 18	ὅτι ἔλεγον ὑμῖν, ὅτι ἐν ἐσχάτῳ χρόνῳ ἔσονται ἐμπαῖκται, κατὰ τὰς ἑαυτῶν ἐπιθυμίας πορευόμενοι τῶν ἀσεβειῶν.	ὅτι ἔλεγον ὑμῖν [ὅτι] Ἐπ' ἐσχάτου [τοῦ] χρόνου ἔσονται ἐμπαῖκται κατὰ τὰς ἑαυτῶν ἐπιθυμίας πορευόμενοι τῶν ἀσεβειῶν.	ὅτι ἔλεγον ὑμῖν ἐπ' ἐσχάτου χρόνου ἔσονται ἐμπαῖκται κατὰ τὰς ἑαυτῶν ἐπιθυμίας πορευόμενοι τῶν ἀσεβειῶν.	o	o	o	o	o

BIBLIOGRAPHY

The King James (Authorized) Version of the Holy Bible.

"1Samuel 15:29 - H5331." *Textus Receptus* Bibles. Accessed on July 08, 2020. http://www.textusreceptusbibles.com/Strongs/9015029/H5331.

"225: ἀλήθεια." GreekLexicon.org. Accessed on July 13, 2020. https://greeklexicon.org/lexicon/strongs/225.

"ABBREVIATIONS & DEFINITIONS." The Dean Burgon Society. Accessed on March 30. http://deanburgonsociety.org/Preservation/miracle.htm.

Aland, Barbara, Kurt Aland, Johannes Karavidopoulos, Carlo M. Martini, Bruce M. Metzger, Eberhard Nestle, and Erwin Nestle. *Nestle-Aland Greek New Testament*, 28th Edition. Stuttgart, Germany: Deutsche Bibelgesellschaft, 2012.

Aland, Kurt and Barbara Aland. *The Text of the New Testament: As Introduction to the Critical Editions and to the Theory and Practice of Textual Criticism*. 2nd Edition. Translated by Erroll F. Rhodes. Grand Rapids, Michigan: William B. Eerdmans Publishing Co., 1989.

Andrews, Edward D. *THE KING JAMES BIBLE: Why Have Modern Why Have Modern Bible Translations Removed Many Verses That Are In the King James Version?* Cambridge, Ohio: Christian Publishing House, 2019.

Barrett, Matthew. *God's Word Alone: The Authority of Scripture*. ePub Edition. Grand Rapids, Michigan: Zondervan, 2016.

Belt, Henk van den. *The Authority of Scripture in Reformed Theology: Truth and Trust*. Leiden, Boston: Brill, 2008.

Brandenburg, Kent. Ed. *Thou Shalt Keep Them*. El Sobrante, California: Pillar & Ground Publishing, 2003.

Brown, F., S. Driver, and C. Briggs. *The Brown-Driver-Briggs Hebrew and English Lexicon*. Peabody: Hendrickson Publishers, 1996.

Burgon, John W. *The Revision Revised: A Refutation of Westcott and Hort's False Greek Text and Theory*. Collingswood, New Jersey: Dean Burgon Society Press, 1883.

Calvin, John. *Commentaries on the Four Last Books of Moses Arranged in the Form of a Harmony*. Grand Rapids, Michigan: Baker Book House, 1984.

Castleman, Robbie F. *Interpreting the God-Breathed Word: How to Read and Study the Bible*. Grand Rapid, MI: Baker Academic, 2018.

Clayton, Robert E. *All Scripture Advocate*. Maitland, FL; Xulon Press, 2003.

Cloud, David W. *The Bible Version Question-Answer Database: Answering the Myths Promoted by Modern Version Defenders*. Port Huron, Michigan: Way of Life Literature, 2005.

Cloud, David W. *What About Ruckman?* Oak Harbor, Washington: Way of Life Literature, 1995.

Clowney. E. P. *Preaching Christ in All Scriptures*. Wheaton, Illinois: Crossway Books, 2003.

Combs, William W. *The Preservation of Scripture*. Detroit Baptist Seminary Journal 5, Fall 2000.

Comfort, Philip W. *Essential Guide to Bible Versions*. Wheaton, Illinois: Tyndale House Publishers, 2000.

Custer, Stewart. *Does Inspiration Demand Inerrancy? A Study of the Biblical Doctrine of Inspiration in the Light of Inerrancy*. Nutley, New Jersey: the Craig Press, 1968.

"Dean Burgon Oath." Far Eastern Bible College. Accessed on February 06, 2020. https://www.febc.edu.sg/v15/article/def_the_dean_burgon_oath.

"Definition of Verbal Plenary Preservation (VPP)." Far Eastern Bible College. Accessed on March 29, 2020. https://www.febc.edu.sg/v15/article/verbal_plenary_preservation.

"Deuteronomy 12:32 - H8104." *Textus Receptus* Bibles. Accessed on July 8, 2020. http://www.textusreceptusbibles.com/Strongs/5012032/H8104.

DOCTRINE/VERBAL PLENARY PRESERVATION. "THE VERBAL PLENARY PRESERATION OF THE SACRED SCRIPTURES." Far Eastern Bible College. Accessed on January 10, 2020. Re-accessed on July 10, 2020. https://www.febc.edu.sg/v15/article/verbal_plenary_preservation.

Eio, Tze Liang Samuel. *Towards A Historical Understanding Of The Doctrine Of Biblical Preservation*. Master's thesis, Far Eastern Bible College, 2014.

Ellis, Robert Ray. *Learning to Read Biblical Hebrew: An Introductory Grammar*. Waco, Texas: Baylor University Press, 2006.

Epp, Eldon Jay and Gordon D. Fee. *Studies in the Theory and Method of New Testament Textual Criticism*. Grand Rapids, Michigan: William B. Eerdmans Publishing Company, 1993.

Ferguson, P. S. "The Historic Views of the Church Concerning Preservation." Confessional Bibliology. Accessed on January 10, 2020.

https://confessionalbibliology.com/wp-content/uploads/2016/04/pb-preservation-quotes.pdf.

Finegan, Jack. *Encountering New Testament Manuscripts: A Working Introduction to Textual Criticism*. Grand Rapids, Michigan: William B. Eerdmans Publishing Company, 1980.

"G225." e-Sword desktop-based Bible software.

George, Calvin. "The Danger of Ruckmanism as Applied to Foreign Language Bibles." LITERATURA BAUTISTA. Accessed on September 03, 2020. https://en.literaturabautista.com/danger-ruckmanism.

Gesenius, Wilhelm. *Gesenius' Hebrew Grammar*. Edited & enlarged by E. Kautzsch. 2nd English edition by A. E. Cowley from the 28th German edition. New York: Oxford University Press, 1910.

Gesenius, Wilhelm. *Gesenius' Hebrew Grammar.* Translated from the 11th German edition by T. J. Conant. Boston: Gould, Kendall, and Lincoln, 1839.

Gesenius, William. *A Hebrew and English Lexicon of the Old Testament: Including the Biblical Chaldee*. 10th edition. By Edward Robinson. Boston: Crocker and Brewster, 1859.

Green, Jay P. Unholy Hands on the Bible, Volume II: An Examination of the Six Major New Versions. Lafayette, Indiana: Sovereign Grace Trust Fund, 1992.

"H571." e-Sword desktop-based Bible software.

Harris, R. Laird. *Introductory Hebrew Grammar*. Grand Rapids, Michigan: WM. B. Eerdmans Publishing Company, 1950.

Hauser, Alan J. and Duane F. Watson. *A History of Biblical Interpretation. Volume 2: The Medieval through the Reformation Periods*. Edited. Grand Rapids, Michigan: William B. Eerdmans Publishing Company, 2009.

Hengstenberg, E. W. *Christology of the Old Testament*. Grand Rapids, Michigan: Kregel Publications, 1970.

Hills, Edward F. *The King James Version Defended*. Des Moines, Iowa: The Christian Research Press, 1984.

"History of the Nestle-Aland Edition." Nestle-Aland Novum Testamentum Braece. Accessed on July 14, 2020. https://www.nestle-aland.com/en/history.

Hostetter, Edwin C. *An Elementary Grammar of Biblical Hebrew*. England: Sheffield Academic Press, 2000.

Houdmann, S. Michael. *Questions about the Bible: The 100 Most Frequently Asked Questions about the Bible*. Edited. Edinburgh, Scotland: WestBow Press, 2015.

"Immutable." Merriam-Webster. Accessed on June 25, 2020. https://www.merriam-webster.com/dictionary/immutability.

"Ἰωτα/Matthew 5:18." *Textus Receptus* Bibles. Accessed on March 29, 2020. http://www.textusreceptusbibles.com/Strongs/40005018/G2503.

Keil C.F. and F. Delitzsch. *Commentary on the Old Testament*. New Zealand: Titus Books, 2014.

"Κεραια/Matthew 5:18." *Textus Receptus* Bibles. Accessed on March 29, 2020. http://www.textusreceptusbibles.com/Strongs/40005018/G2762.

Khoo, Jeffrey. *Charismatism Q&A: Biblical Answers to Frequently Asked Questions on the Charismatic Phenomenon*. Singapore: Far Eastern Bible College Press, 1999.

__________. *Greek Exegesis I: Lecture Note*. Singapore: Far Eastern Bible College, 2019.

__________. *Kept Pure in All Ages*. Singapore: Far Eastern Bible College Press, 2001.

__________. *KJV Questions & Answer*. Singapore: Bible Witness Literature Ministry, 2003.

Kwon, Hyeonik. *The History of the Ture Church before the 16th-Century Reformation*. Seoul, Korea: Seum Books, 2019.

Lasor, William S., David A. Hubbard, and Frederic W. Bush. *Old Testament Survey: The Message, Form, and Background of the Old Testament*. Grand Rapids, Michigan: William B. Eerdmans Publishing Company, 1982.

Lenski, R. C. H. *The Interpretation of St. Matthew's Gospel*. Minneapolis, Minnesota: Augsburg Publishing House, 1943.

Lewis, Gordon R. *Testing Christianity's Truth Claims: Approaches to Christian Apologetics*. Chicago, Illinois: Moody Press, 1976.

Lin, Yii-Jan. *The Erotic Life of Manuscripts: New Testament Textual Criticism and the Biological Sciences*. New York, NY: Oxford University Press, 2016.

MacArthur, John F. *Nothing but the Truth: Upholding the Gospel in a Doubting Age*. Wheaton, Illinois: Crossway Books, 1999.

__________. *The MacArthur New Testament Commentary*. Nashville, Tennessee: Thomas Nelson Publishers, 2007.

__________. *The Truth War: Fighting for Certainty in an Age of Deception*. Nashville, Tennessee: Thomas Nelson, 2007.

Machen, J. Gresham. *Christianity and Liberalism*. Grand Rapids, Michigan: WM. B. Eerdmans Publishing Company, 1923.

__________. *The Christian View of Man*. Carlisle, Pennsylvania: The Banner of Truth Trust, 1937.

Manton, M. E. *A Dictionary of Theological Terms*. London, U.K.: Grace Publications, 1996.

Metzger, Bruce M. and Bart D. Ehrman. *The Text of New Testament*. New York, Oxford: Oxford University Press, 2005.

Moorman, Jack. *8,000 Differences Between the N.T. Greek Words of the King James Bible and the Modern Versions*. London, England: The Old Paths Publications, Inc., 2008.

Muller, Richard A. *Dictionary of Latin and Greek Theological Terms*. Grand Rapid, MI: Baker Book House, 1985.

"Nestle Aland." Theopedia. Accessed on October 10, 2021. https://www.theopedia.com/nestle-aland.

Nicole, Roger. "The Biblical Concept of Truth." D. A. Carson and John D. Woodbridge, Edited. *Scripture and Truth*. Grand Rapids, Michigan: Baker Book House, 1992.

"Νόμοσ/Matthew 5:18." *Textus Receptus* Bibles. Accessed on March 29. http://www.textusreceptusbibles.com/Strongs/40005018/G3551.

Paché, René. *The Inspiration and Authority of Scripture*. Chicago: Moody Press, 1969.

"Plenary." Merriam-Webster. Accessed on May 07, 2020. https://www.merriam-webster.com/dictionary/plenary.

Porter, Stanley E. and Andrew W. Pitts. *Fundamentals of New Testament Textual Criticism*. Grand Rapids, Michigan: William B. Eerdmans Publishing Company, 2015.

Price, James D. *King James Onlyism: A New Sect*. Chattanooga, Tennessee: James D. Price Publisher, 2006.

"Psalm 12:7." Bible Gateway. Accessed on March 30, 2020. https://www.biblegateway.com.

Rov, G. John. *Concealed from Christians for the Glory of God: The 1611 KJV - The King James Bible Authorized Version*. Morrisville, US: Lulu Press, Inc., 2019.

Ruckman, Peter S. "Advanced Revelations in the King's English." *Bible Believers' Bulletin*, vol.33 no.1. Pensacola, Florida: Bible Baptist Church, January 2009.

______________. "The Super Superiority of the King James Bible." *Bible Believers' Bulletin*, vol.32 no.2. Pensacola, Florida: Bible Baptist Church, February 2008.

"Rules of Textual Criticism." Bible Research. Accessed on March 18, 2020. http://www.bible-researcher.com/rules.html.

Ryrie, Charles C. *A Survey of Bible Doctrine*. Chicago: Moody Publishers, 1972.

SEE THE MANUSCRIPT. "2 Peter 3:10." Codex Sinaiticus. Accessed on November 27, 2021. http://www.codex-sinaiticus.net/en/manuscript.aspx?book=54&chapter=3&lid=en&side=r&verse=10&zoomSlider=0.

Shin, Young Gil. "God's Promise to Preserve His Word: an Exegetical Study of Psalm 12:5-7." Master's thesis, Far Eastern Bible College, 1999.

Shorter Catechism of the Assembly of Divines. "WESTMINSTER SHORTER CATECHISM: WITH PROOF TEXT." A Puritan's Mind. Accessed on December 23, 2019. http://www.reformed.org/documents/wsc/index.html?_top=http://www.reformed.org/documents/WSC.html.

Shorter Oxford English Dictionary on Historical Principles: Volume 1 •A-M. 5th Edition. Oxford, U.K.: Oxford University Press, 2002.

Skariah, George. "The Biblical Doctrine of the Perfect Preservation of the Holy Scriptures." PhD diss., Far Eastern Bible College Press, 2005.

Standish, Colin D. and Russell R. Standish. *The Perils of Ecumenism*. Rapidan, Virginia: Hartland Publications, 2003.

Streeter, Lloyd L. *Seventy-five Problems: with Central Baptist Seminary's Book – The Bible Version Debate*. Lasalle, IL: First Baptist Church of LaSalle, 2001.

Tenney, Merrill C. *New Testament Survey*. Revised by Walter M. Dunnett. Grand Rapids, Michigan: WM. B. Eerdmans publishing Company, 1985.

Thayer, Joseph H. *Thayer's Greek-English Lexicon of the New Testament*. Grand Rapids, Michigan: Baker Book House, 1977.

"The difference between Immutable and Inalterable." DiffSense. Accessed on June 26, 2020. https://diffsense.com/diff/immutable/inalterable.

"The History of the Textus Receptus." Textus Receptus Bibles. Accessed on October 10, 2021. http://textusreceptusbibles.com/History.

Tow, Timothy. *The Clock of the Sevenfold Will of God*. Singapore: Far Eastern Bible College Press, 1991.

"Truth." Cambridge Dictionary. Accessed on May 10, 2020. https://dictionary.cambridge.org/dictionary/english/truth.

"Truth." Merriam-Webster. Accessed on May 10, 2020. https://www.merriam-webster.com/dictionary/truth.

"Inalterable vs. Unalterable," AskDifference, accessed on April 12, 2022, https://www.askdifference.com/inalterable-vs-unalterable.

"Verbal." Dictionary.com. Accessed on March 29, 2020. https://www.dictionary.com/browse/verbal.

"Verbal." Merriam-Webster. Accessed on May 07, 2020. https://www.merriam-webster.com/dictionary/verbal.

Waite, D. A. *Defending the King James Bible*. Collingswood, New Jersey: The Bible for Today Press, 1996.

Wallace, Daniel B. *Greek Grammar Beyond the Basics: An Exegetical Syntax of the New Testament with Scripture, Subject, and Greek Word Indexes*. Grand Rapids, Michigan: Zondervan Academic, 1997.

Wallace, Daniel B. and Grant G. Edward. *New Testament Syntax*. Grand Rapids, Michigan: Zondervan, 2007.

Waltke, Bruce K. *An Old Testament Theology: An Exegetical, Canonical, and Thematic Approach*. Grand Rapids, Michigan: Zondervan Academic, 2007.

Wasserman, Tommy and Peter J. Gurry. *A New Approach to Textual Criticism: An Introduction to the Coherence-Based Genealogical Method*. Atlanta, GA: Society of Biblical Literature, 2017; Stuttgart, Germany: Deutsche Bibelgesellschaft, 2017.

Wegner, Paul D. *A Student's Guide to Textual Criticism of the Bible: Its History, Methods and Results*. Downers Grove, Illinois: InterVarsity Press, 2006.

Wenham, J. W. *The Elements of New Testament Greek*. Cambridge, UK: Cambridge University Press, 1965.

Webster, Noah. *Webster's New Twentieth Century Dictionary*. Unabridged 2nd Edition. Edited by J. L. McKechine. Collins World, Cleveland: William Collins Publishers, Inc., 1979.

"Westminster Confession of Faith Chapter 1: Of the Holy Scripture - no.4." Bible Presbyterian Church General Synod. Accessed on March 22, 2020. https://bpc.org/?page_id=542.

"Westminster Confession of Faith Chapter 1: Of the Holy Scripture - no.8." Bible Presbyterian Church General Synod. Accessed on March 29, 2020. Re-accessed on July 10, 2020. https://bpc.org/?page_id=542.

"Westminster Shorter Catechism - Q4." Bible Presbyterian Church General Synod. Accessed July 07, 2020. Re-accessed on July 13, 2020. https://bpc.org/?page_id=341.

"Westminster Shorter Catechism - Q14." Bible Presbyterian Church General Synod. Accessed July 12, 2020. https://bpc.org/?page_id=341.

Williams, H. D. *The Miracle of Biblical Inspiration*. Cleveland, Georgia: The Old Paths Publications Inc., 2009.

Williams, Ronald J. *Williams' Hebrew Syntax*. 3rd ed. Toronto, Canada: University of Toronto Press, 2007.

**Dr. Ra ChaeWon
and husband, Dr. S. K. Park**

PhD in Business Administration (2007)
- Master of Divinity (2020)
- A Candidate for the Master of Theology (as of April 2022)

Dr. Ra ChaeWon earned her PhD in Business Administration from Yonsei University in Seoul, South Korea in 2007. From September 2010 to December 2016, she had served as an accounting professor at Handong Global University in Pohang, South Korea. Afterwards, in response to God's calling for her with John 21:18, she joined Far Eastern Bible College in Singapore in 2017 for her theological studies. She earned her Master of Divinity in 2020 and is currently working on her thesis for Master of Theology.

Rev. Dr. Park SeungKyu, her husband, received his PhD in History from Kyunghee University in Seoul, South Korea; and also Doctor of Theology from Far Eastern Bible College in Singapore. He has served as the principal of the Bible College of East Africa Tanzania since 2014, and Dr. Ra ChaeWon also joined the same college in 2020 to serve as a professor. Both are missionaries belonging to the True Life Bible Presbyterian Church in Singapore as well as the Independent Board for Presbyterian Foreign Missions in the United States.

Their two lovely God-given daughters, like their parents, are currently studying theology at Far Eastern Bible College. Their first daughter, Park JongHwi (Angela), is now studying for her Master of Divinity; and their younger daughter, Park JongEun (Joyce), is for Bachelor of Theology.

Far Eastern Bible College

Far Eastern Bible College in Singapore was established in 1962, inheriting the tradition of Bible Presbyterians in the United States who defended the Word of God and adhered to biblical separation based on the Word. She followed the same steps as Dr. Carl McIntire, who was a leading fighter for faith and the Word, and spurred its establishment with the help of the Independent Board for Presbyterian Foreign Missions of the United States. Following the founding principal, Rev. Dr. Timothy Tow, Rev. Dr. Jeffrey Khoo is now in charge of Far Eastern Bible College as her second principal.

At Far Eastern Bible College, the written Word of God comes first, second and third. It is a 'Bible College' that practices *"Quod non est biblicum, non est theologicum"* by thoroughly educating the Word itself before theology. In particular, the original languages of Hebrew and Greek together with the traditional texts (the Hebrew Masoretic Text for the Old Testament and the Greek *Textus Receptus* for the New Testament) are very intensively taught for at least three years. Thus, her graduates who successfully pass these three-full-year intensive courses will be equipped with the basic qualifications to expound directly from the original Hebrew and Greek Scriptures themselves.

Bible College of East Africa: Kenya, Tanzania, and Rwanda

Bible College of East Africa was established in Nairobi, Kenya by the Independent Board for Presbyterian Foreign Missions of the United States in 1965. After that, as Rev. Dr.

Mark Kim joined as her principal, Korean missionaries began to get involved in earnest. Following the first and main campus in Kenya, the second campus was established in Usa River, Tanzania in 2006, and the third campus in Kigali, Rwanda in 2017.

Most of her faculty members (who are also missionaries) graduated from Far Eastern Bible College in Singapore. Thus, they can have been teaching and nurturing students in the same doctrinal stance toward God and His Word. Currently, the Kenya and Rwanda campuses are headed by Rev. Dr. Mark Kim, and the Tanzania campus by Rev. Dr. Park SeungKyu.